This Cookbook
Belongs To

Kids Cookies

Scrumptious Recipes for Bakers Ages 9 to 13

GENERAL EDITOR
CHUCK WILLIAMS

CONCEPT, RECIPES & TEXT
SUSAN MANLIN KATZMAN

PHOTOGRAPHY
CHRIS SHORTEN

TIME
LIFE
BOOKS

TIME-LIFE BOOKS

Time-Life Books is a division of Time Life Inc.
Time-Life is a trademark of Time Warner Inc. U.S.A.

Time-Life Custom Publishing

Vice President and Publisher: Terry Newell
Vice President of Sales and Marketing: Neil Levin
Director of Financial Operations: J. Brian Birky
Director of Acquisitions: Jennifer L. Pearce

WILLIAMS-SONOMA

Founder and Vice Chairman: Chuck Williams
Associate Book Buyer: Cecilia Michaelis

WELDON OWEN INC.

President: John Owen
Vice President and Publisher: Wendely Harvey
Chief Financial Officer: Larry Partington
Vice President International Sales: Stuart Laurence
Managing Editor: Val Cipollone
Consulting Editor: Norman Kolpas
Copy Editor: Sharon Silva
Design: Patty Hill
Production Director: Stephanie Sherman
Production Consultant: Sarah Lemas
Production Manager: Jen Dalton
Production Editor: Deborah Cowder
Food Photographer: Chris Shorten
Food Stylist: Heidi Gintner
Step-by-step Photographer: Brian Pierce
Step-by-step Food Stylist: Kim Konecny
Assistant Food Stylist: Shirin Ferdinand
Prop Stylist: Thea Geck

The Williams-Sonoma Kitchen Library
conceived and produced by Weldon Owen Inc.
814 Montgomery St., San Francisco, CA 94133

In collaboration with Williams-Sonoma
3250 Van Ness Ave., San Francisco, CA 94109

Production by Toppan Printing Co., (HK) Ltd.
Printed in China

The publisher and the author have made every
effort to emphasize the importance of safety
procedures when children are baking in the
kitchen. Neither the publisher nor the author
can assume responsibility for any accident,
injuries, losses, or other damages resulting from
the use of this book. Children should not use
this cookbook without adult supervision.

A Weldon Owen Production

Copyright © 1998 Weldon Owen Inc.
Reprinted in 1999, 2000
All rights reserved, including the right of
reproduction in whole or in part in any form.

Library of Congress
Cataloging-in-Publication Data:

Kids cookies : scrumptious recipes for bakers ages 9 to 13 / general
    editor, Chuck Williams ; concept, recipes & text, Susan Manlin
    Katzman ; photography, Chris Shorten.
        p.   cm.
    Includes index.
    Summary : Presents instructions for making a variety of cookies,
including iced buttery cutouts, chocolate chip cookies, double-fudge
brownies, and jelly thumbprints.
    ISBN 0-7370-2008-3
    1. Cookies—Juvenile literature.   [1. Cookies. 2. Baking.]
I. Williams, Chuck.   II. Katzman, Susan Manlin.   III. Shorten,
Chris, ill.
TX772.K533   1998
641.8'654—DC21   98-14974
                                                               CIP
                                                               AC

Contents

ROLLED & CUT COOKIES 20

DROP COOKIES 39

BAR COOKIES & BROWNIES 54

SHAPED COOKIES 77

INTRODUCTION

You may not believe it, but when I was a boy growing up in northern Florida in the 1920s there was no such thing as chocolate chip cookies. (They were actually invented around 1930 at the Toll House Inn in Massachusetts, which is why some people still call them Toll House cookies.)

Still, my sister and I enjoyed making all sorts of other cookies. My favorites were crisp sugar cookies, the kind you could cut into shapes with cookie cutters and then decorate with cinnamon-sugar or icing. Then we graduated to icebox cookies. Almost every day after school, I rushed to the refrigerator to take out that log of chilled dough and slice cookies to bake for a snack or an after-dinner dessert.

Apart from the popularity of chocolate chip cookies, nothing much has changed after all those years. Kids still love to make cookies, because cookies are still easy, fun, and delicious.

Easy, fun, and delicious also describe the recipes Susan Manlin Katzman has created for this book. She has spent many years teaching children how to cook, so she knows what children like.

Flip through these pages now and you'll see an incredible variety of treats that any kid can learn to make. Preparing them is even easier, thanks to the basic instructions on the pages that follow. Please read through them before you start. Pay close attention to the safety guidelines on pages 6–7. It's also a good idea to go over these with a parent or other adult to make sure you understand this important information, especially because making cookies involves working with very hot ovens and baking sheets.

Then pick out a recipe and get started. I guarantee you'll have a lot of fun. And you'll probably learn something, too, although, unlike homework, the results are good enough to eat!

Chuck Williams

Chuck Williams, Susan Manlin Katzman, and busy young bakers

4

❦ SAFETY FIRST

Baking is great fun, but it can sometimes be dangerous. Good bakers use caution and always put safety first. Follow these easy tips and you'll become a super-and safe-baker.

BEFORE YOU START BAKING

✓ **Get an adult's permission to bake.** Even after you've learned the safe way to bake, never start baking until you have permission from a parent or other grown-up. Bake only when an adult is home and able to help out with questions or problems.

✓ **Take a tour of your kitchen.** Make sure you know how to use all the equipment and electrical appliances you'll need to cook and bake. If you don't know, ask an adult. Also find out what to do in case of a fire, where the fire extinguisher is, and how to use it. (This is very important. See the box titled In Case of Fire on the opposite page.)

✓ **Wear an apron to keep your clothes clean.** And wash your hands with warm water and soap before you start baking.

✓ **Start out and stay neat.** Neatness will help you avoid accidents. Plan a place and clear a space to work in your kitchen. Keep everything neat while you're working. As soon as something drops or spills, wipe up the mess.

✓ **Keep everything clear of the oven and the stove's burners.** Roll up your sleeves and tie back long hair. Keep track of pot holders, recipes, kitchen towels, and cookbooks, placing them well away from the oven and the stove top.

WHILE YOU'RE BAKING

✓ **Turn off a mixer's motor before reaching in the mixing bowl.** Never reach into the mixing bowl with your hand or try to scrape the sides of the bowl with a spatula while the mixer is still running.

✓ **Turn off a blender's motor before removing the lid.** Never try to stir the contents or scrape the sides of the blender while the motor is on.

✓ *Never* **use wet hands to turn on a switch or pull out or push in a plug.** Dry your hands completely before touching anything electrical.

✓ **Turn off the heat before removing a pan from the burner.**

✓ **Use only dry pot holders.** If you pick up something hot with a wet pot holder, you'll get a nasty burn. Heat travels quickly through water and dampness.

✓ **Carefully remove hot baking sheets and pans from the oven.** First, have your hot pads or cooling racks in place on your counter. Then, carefully open the oven door. Using pot holders, firmly grasp the baking sheet or pan with both hands and transfer it to the hot pad or rack. Carefully close the oven door. If you wear glasses, be prepared: the heat from the oven might make the lenses foggy.

✓ **Keep pots and pans away from the edge of the counter.** That way, passersby can't bump into them and get burned.

✓**Don't position pan handles over hot burners.** They can pick up the heat and burn your hand.

✓**Don't leave the kitchen in mid-recipe.** Never walk out while something is in a mixer, in the oven, or on the stove. Always stay in charge and keep an eye on the action.

✓**Use fresh, high-quality ingredients.** Food always tastes best when made with the freshest ingredients. Be aware of "use by" dates on packages, especially on dairy products and eggs, and use the food within the given time limit.

✓**Always wash your hands thoroughly after handling food.**

KNIVES AND OTHER SHARP TOOLS

✓**Never hold ingredients in your hand when cutting.** Put the ingredients on a cutting board.

✓**Hold knives firmly and handle with care.** Keep a good grip on the handle and cut with the blade pointing away from you. Keep your fingers well clear of the blade.

✓**Use sharp tools only for the required job.** At other times, keep them stored safely away. Don't clown around with knives: no way are they for play.

✓**Walk, don't run.** Always move cautiously when holding sharp tools.

✓**Wash sharp tools individually.** During cleanup, never put them in soapy water. You might forget they're there and grab a blade or a sharp edge by mistake.

IN CASE OF FIRE

If you are careful in the kitchen, you'll probably never have to deal with a fire. But fires do happen: from a faulty electrical appliance or a kitchen towel left too near a burner. Read this information carefully with an adult.

✓**Call for help.** Don't try to handle a fire alone. Call for help immediately.

✓**Know your fire extinguisher.** Every kitchen should have one. Know where it is stored and how to use it.

✓**Smothering a small pan fire.** If the fire is contained within a pan on the stove, it is most likely a grease fire. DO NOT PUT WATER ON IT! Turn off the heat immediately. Smother the flames by placing a tight-fitting lid on the pan. *Never* try to move a pan with a fire in it.

✓**Smothering an oven fire.** If the fire is contained within the oven, turn off the oven immediately without opening the oven door. Smother the flames by keeping the door shut.

✓**Extinguishing other small fires.** If there is a small fire someplace other than in the oven or on the stove and it is not spreading quickly, use your fire extinguisher to put out the flames immediately.

✓**Larger fires.** If a fire is bigger than the size of a saucepan or is spreading quickly, do not try to fight it yourself. Warn everyone in the house by yelling "FIRE!" and get everyone out of the house at once. Call the fire department from a neighbor's house.

STAY ALERT AND YOU WON'T GET HURT.

☞ EQUIPMENT

The equipment, big and small, that you need to make the recipes in this book

Having the right equipment in your kitchen makes baking easy. Before starting to bake, check a recipe's equipment list to make sure you have everything listed. Remember that good-quality kitchen equipment is easy and safe to use, gives you good results, and will last longer. Take good care of all your equipment. Wash and dry it carefully, and store it where it won't get damaged.

POTS & PANS

Heavy baking sheets
Flat metal sheets hold cookies while they bake in the oven. A sheet with two or three rimless sides makes it easier to remove cookies.

Large baking pan
Pan with 1-inch sides for baking bar cookies.

Baking dishes and pans
Heatproof glass, earthenware, or metal containers are useful for bar cookies and brownies.

Cake pan
Square metal pan is perfect for baking brownies and bar cookies.

Pizza pan
Round metal tray holds a sweet pizza while it bakes in the oven.

Springform pan
Cake pan with removable sides makes it easy to handle delicate baked goods.

Saucepan
Pan for stove-top cooking such as melting butter.

Wooden spoon
Because they don't get hot, wooden spoons with long handles are the best choice for stirring foods while they cook.

Icing spatula
Small, flexible blade for spreading icing.

Rubber spatula
For scraping the sides of mixing bowls.

Large metal spatula
For transferring unbaked and baked cookies from one surface to another.

Pastry brushes
For brushing glazes on dough.

Sieve
For making dry ingredients powdery smooth, such as a fine dust of confectioners' sugar.

Pot holders
Thick, heavy-duty cotton protects hands when handling hot pots or pans.

Hot pad
Got a hot pot or pan? Put it down on this quilted pad and it won't burn the kitchen counter.

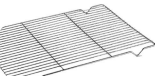

Cooling rack
Lets air circulate under hot baking sheets and pans of cookies so they'll cool more quickly.

Mixing bowls
For mixing and stirring all kinds of ingredients.

Electric mixer
Handheld mixer with different speeds quickly mixes batters and doughs.

Box grater
For grating citrus zest into small and very small pieces.

Rolling pin
Lets you roll out cookie dough perfectly flat, just like a professional baker.

Cookie cutters
Press into cookie dough to create all kinds of shapes.

Cookie press
For pressing cookie dough into patterned shapes.

Piping bag and tips
For writing and decorating with icing.

How to Measure Ingredients

In baking, careful measuring can make the difference between "Wow!" and "Ugh!" So you'll want to know and practice the techniques explained here. Once you do, your baking will measure up to the best in town.

TOOLS FOR MEASURING

Cups for Measuring Liquids
Cups used to measure liquids are transparent so you can line up the top of the liquid with the measurements marked on the side. They can be made of glass or plastic.

Cups for Measuring Dry Ingredients
Dry-ingredient measuring cups hold an exact amount and have straight rims so you can level off the ingredients. They are usually made of metal or plastic. The most common sizes are ¼ cup, ⅓ cup, ½ cup, and 1 cup.

Spoons for Measuring Liquid and Dry Ingredients
These spoons are used to measure exact, small amounts of both dry and liquid ingredients. The most common sizes are ¼ teaspoon, ½ teaspoon, 1 teaspoon, and 1 tablespoon. Their rims are straight so you can level off dry ingredients precisely. Measuring spoons are made of metal or plastic.

TO MEASURE LIQUID INGREDIENTS

Place the liquid measuring cup on a flat surface. Move in close to the cup so you can see the exact line of measurement you will be using. Slowly pour in the liquid until you reach the line. Check the measurement at eye level to make sure it's exact.

TO MEASURE DRY INGREDIENTS

Spoon dry ingredients such as flour and sugar into the proper-size measuring cup, loosely heaping it into the cup. (Don't pack the ingredient into the cup unless you are measuring brown sugar; brown sugar is always firmly packed into cups.) Level the ingredient by running the straight edge of a knife or a spatula over the top of the cup.

TO USE MEASURING SPOONS

Use the same type measuring spoons for dry and liquid ingredients. Always measure away from bowls or pans, so any accidental spills won't mix with other ingredients. Scoop up or heap dry ingredients into the spoon. Then use the blunt edge of a knife or a  spatula to level it off. For a liquid, slowly pour it into the spoon until it fills to the rim. For sticky ingredients like honey or peanut butter, use a rubber scraper to scrape them out of the spoon.

TO MEASURE BUTTER

Butter comes in sticks with measurements marked right on the paper wrapper. Most sticks are $1/2$ cup, and the markings divide them up into 8 tablespoons. To get the exact amount you need, use a small, sharp knife to cut straight down through the paper along the correct line.

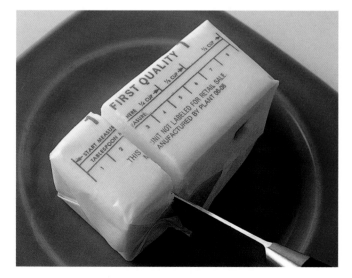

KITCHEN MATH

dash = 2 or 3 drops

pinch = amount you can pick up between your thumb and forefinger

3 teaspoons = 1 tablespoon

4 tablespoons = $1/4$ cup

5 tablespoons + 1 teaspoon = $1/3$ cup

1 cup = 8 fluid ounces

2 cups = 1 pint

2 pints = 1 quart

4 quarts = 1 gallon

4 ounces = $1/4$ pound

8 ounces = $1/2$ pound

12 ounces = $3/4$ pound

16 ounces = 1 pound

How to Follow a Recipe

If you are new to baking, you need to understand how to follow a recipe. Read these easy steps, look over the sample recipe below, and you'll be ready to start baking.

READY, SET...

1 **Read the recipe before you begin.** Make sure you read every word of it and understand exactly what you will be doing, how to do it, and about how much time you will need. If you don't understand some words, check the Glossary on page 106, the Equipment guide on page 8, or ask an adult. Check your clock to make sure you have enough time to finish what you start.

2 **Clear a work space.** The less clutter, the less chance that you will make a mistake.

3 **Get your equipment ready.** Set out all equipment and utensils needed for the recipe. Make sure that pans and bowls are the same sizes the recipe suggests.

4 **Gather all ingredients.** Check the recipe's ingredient list and gather everything around your work space. Carefully measure out what you'll need and set the measured ingredients aside. Wash any fresh fruits under cold running water.

5 **Start baking!**

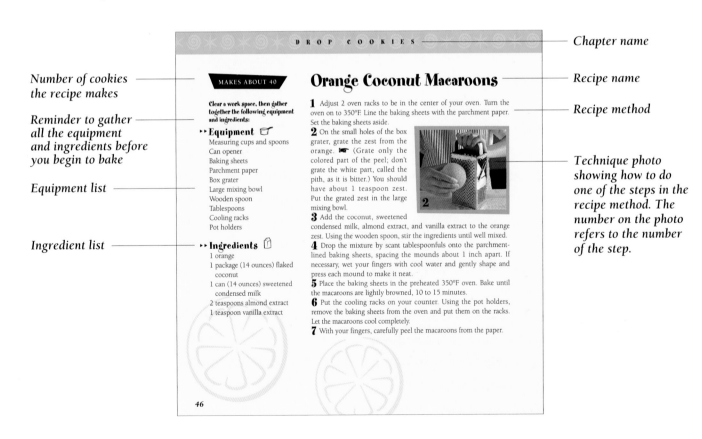

Number of cookies the recipe makes

Reminder to gather all the equipment and ingredients before you begin to bake

Equipment list

Ingredient list

Chapter name

Recipe name

Recipe method

Technique photo showing how to do one of the steps in the recipe method. The number on the photo refers to the number of the step.

DROP COOKIES

MAKES ABOUT 40

Clear a work space, then gather together the following equipment and ingredients:

Equipment
Measuring cups and spoons
Can opener
Baking sheets
Parchment paper
Box grater
Large mixing bowl
Wooden spoon
Tablespoons
Cooling racks
Pot holders

Ingredients
1 orange
1 package (14 ounces) flaked coconut
1 can (14 ounces) sweetened condensed milk
2 teaspoons almond extract
1 teaspoon vanilla extract

Orange Coconut Macaroons

1 Adjust 2 oven racks to be in the center of your oven. Turn the oven on to 350°F. Line the baking sheets with the parchment paper. Set the baking sheets aside.

2 On the small holes of the box grater, grate the zest from the orange. ☛ (Grate only the colored part of the peel; don't grate the white part, called the pith, as it is bitter.) You should have about 1 teaspoon zest. Put the grated zest in the large mixing bowl.

3 Add the coconut, sweetened condensed milk, almond extract, and vanilla extract to the orange zest. Using the wooden spoon, stir the ingredients until well mixed.

4 Drop the mixture by scant tablespoonfuls onto the parchment-lined baking sheets, spacing the mounds about 1 inch apart. If necessary, wet your fingers with cool water and gently shape and press each mound to make it neat.

5 Place the baking sheets in the preheated 350°F oven. Bake until the macaroons are lightly browned, 10 to 15 minutes.

6 Put the cooling racks on your counter. Using the pot holders, remove the baking sheets from the oven and put them on the racks. Let the macaroons cool completely.

7 With your fingers, carefully peel the macaroons from the paper.

46

G O !

Here are some special tips and hints to help you while you're baking.

✔ **Follow the instructions carefully.** The more care you take to do things exactly as described in the recipe, the better results you'll get.

✔ **Clean up as you work.** Put dirty dishes in the sink and wipe up spills as they occur.

✔ **Chill the dough if it's too soft to work with.** If a dough that you need to roll out or shape by hand is too soft or a bit sticky to handle, put it in the refrigerator until it becomes a bit firmer.

✔ **Make the cookies that you bake on one baking sheet the same size and thickness.** That way all the cookies will bake evenly.

✔ **Adjust the oven racks as each recipe directs.** When a recipe directs you to "adjust two oven racks to be in the center of your oven," put one rack in the upper center (upper third) and the other in the lower center (lower third). Be sure to have two hot pads or two cooling racks ready for the sheets of cookies when they come out of the oven. If you can bake only one sheet of cookies at a time, or if a recipe directs you to do so, put a rack in the center of your oven.

✔ **Check cookies at the minimum baking time.** Set a timer to the minimum time specified in the recipe and it will ring when the time is up. If needed, continue baking the cookies, checking them often until they are done.

✔ **Let baking sheets cool completely before using them again.** If you put dough on a warm baking sheet, it might spread too much.

✔ **Cool cookies in one layer.** Don't stack cookies while they cool, and make sure cookies are completely cool before storing them.

Orange Coconut Macaroons, page 46

Testing baked goods for doneness

In addition to baking times, recipes describe how the cookies you are baking should look and, sometimes, feel when they are done. A recipe will suggest a simple test to check for doneness. You might watch for the first sign of browning around the edges of cookies, or for a dough to become firm or "set." Or you might insert a toothpick into the center of bar cookies in a pan to see if it comes out clean. Your sense of smell is also important. The fragrant aroma of cookies baking is much sweeter than the bitter smell of something that has baked for too long and is burning.

Because no two bakers, ingredients, utensils, or ovens are the same, recipes cannot always be exact. You have to trust your own judgment when baking. If your recipe says to "bake the cookies for 10 to 15 minutes" and you see that they are turning very brown after only 8 minutes, bake the cookies for less time. Trust yourself… and have fun!

Basic Baking Techniques

Safe, easy methods for 12 different baking tasks you'll find yourself doing over and over and over again

Certain baking steps show up in lots of recipes. On the following pages are 12 lessons that every new baker should learn. These skills are used over and over again throughout this book.

Look over the steps carefully now and imagine doing them. The next time a recipe calls for you to grease a pan, separate an egg, or mix a dough with your hands, turn to the appropriate demonstration and follow it. Continue to use the instructions until you can do the steps safely and automatically.

HOW TO BREAK AND SEPARATE AN EGG

1 To break an egg, gently but firmly tap the middle of the egg on the edge of a bowl to crack the shell.

2 Gently pull the shell apart. Let the yolk and white fall into the bowl. Or separate the egg as directed in step 3.

3 To separate an egg, crack the egg as directed in step 1. Carefully pass the yolk back and forth between the shell halves, letting the white fall into a small bowl. Put the yolk into another small bowl.

HOW TO GREASE A PAN

1 Put a little piece of solid shortening or softened butter in the pan. Using a paper towel, rub the shortening or butter all over the inside of the pan to coat the bottom and sides thinly and evenly.

HOW TO CHOP NUTS

1 Put the nuts (here peanuts) on a chopping board. Hold the handle of the knife with one hand. Steady the top of the knife with your other hand. Raise and lower the handle to cut the nuts into pieces. This technique is used to chop other ingredients, too.

HOW TO GRATE CITRUS ZEST

1 Rub the citrus fruit over the small holes of the grater. Grate only the colored part of the skin—the zest. The white part underneath is bitter.

HOW TO BEAT BUTTER, SUGAR, AND EGGS

1 With the electric mixer set at medium-high speed, beat together the butter and the sugar until smooth and creamy, about 2 minutes. Turn off the mixer.

2 Add the eggs and, with the mixer set on medium-high speed, beat the mixture until fluffy, about 2 minutes. Turn off the mixer.

HOW TO SCRAPE A BOWL

1 To mix the ingredients evenly, scrape the bowl from time to time with the edge of a rubber spatula. Always turn the mixer off before you scrape the bowl.

HOW TO BEAT IN FLOUR

1 With the mixer turned off, add the flour and other dry ingredients to the bowl. You'll do this either gradually or all at once, as the recipe directs.

2 With the electric mixer set on low speed, beat in all the dry ingredients until no traces remain, about 2 minutes.

HOW TO MIX DOUGH WITH YOUR HANDS

1 Sometimes a dough is mixed by rubbing the ingredients together with your fingers, just until a crumbly mixture forms. This method makes a dough that's flaky and crisp.

2 Sometimes a dough is mixed by squeezing or pressing the ingredients together with your hands. This method is commonly used when a dough calls for only a few ingredients.

3 Sometimes a dough is mixed by kneading the ingredients together with your hands. Press, fold, and press the dough again. This method is often used for firm doughs.

HOW TO ROLL OUT COOKIE DOUGH

1 Sprinkle a work surface and a rolling pin with flour. Begin rolling out the dough by applying firm, even pressure with the rolling pin. Roll from the center to the edges.

2 Continue rolling out the dough as specified in each recipe. You can measure the dimensions and thickness of the dough with a ruler.

HOW TO ROLL COOKIE DOUGH INTO A BALL OR A LOG

1 Scoop up the amount of dough specified in the recipe. Roll the dough between the palms of your hands to make a ball.

1 Sprinkle a work surface with flour. Roll the dough with your palms to form a log. Make the log as long and as thick as the recipe directs.

1 Attach the top and the handle to the tube of the cookie press. Using a spatula or your hands, put the dough into the tube.

2 Choose the design plate that you would like to use. Screw it into its holder. Screw the holder onto the tube of the cookie press.

3 Hold the press straight up and down. Grip the handle and apply even pressure to press out the cookie dough. Be sure to read all instructions carefully.

HOW TO DROP COOKIE DOUGH

1 Scoop up a spoonful of dough as directed in the recipe. Use another spoon to drop the dough onto a baking sheet.

HOW TO STORE COOKIES

How you store a cookie has a lot to do with what type of cookie it is. Store delicate, crisp cookies in a sturdy container such as a cookie jar or tin. Store softer cookies the same way or in a sturdy plastic bag. It's important that all of these containers have tight-fitting lids or a tight seal. Store bar cookies in the pan that you bake them in, tightly covered with aluminum foil. Don't mix cookies when storing; store each type in its own separate container.

HOW TO MAKE AND USE ICING

Icing is used to frost and decorate all kinds of cookies. Some icing is thick and creamy enough to spread, and some is thin and smooth enough to use for writing and decorating with a piping bag.

Rich and Creamy Icing

▸▸ **Equipment** 🥄 ▸▸ **Ingredients** 🥛

Equipment	Ingredients
Measuring cups and spoons	2 tablespoons unsalted butter
Small saucepan	2 cups confectioners' sugar, or more if needed
Small sieve	1 teaspoon vanilla extract
Medium mixing bowl	2 tablespoons heavy cream, more if needed
Tablespoon	Food coloring in 1 or more different colors (optional)
Electric mixer	
Rubber spatula	
Small bowls (optional)	
Small spoons (optional)	

1 Put the butter in the small saucepan. Set the saucepan on a burner of your stove and turn the heat on to medium. Heat only until the butter melts, then turn off the heat.

2 Hold the sieve over the mixing bowl. Put the confectioners' sugar in the sieve, ½ cup at a time. With the bottom of the tablespoon, press the sugar through the sieve into the bowl. Repeat with the remaining sugar. Add the melted butter, vanilla, and 2 tablespoons cream. With the electric mixer set on medium speed, beat until 🥄 the mixture is creamy and spreadable. If necessary, add more cream to make the icing thinner or more sugar to make the icing stiffer.

3 Use the icing immediately. If you want to tint the icing, add a few drops of food coloring and stir until the mixture 🥄 is evenly colored. You can also divide the icing among a few small bowls and tint each portion a different color.

Makes about ¾ cup

Decorating Icing

▸▸ Equipment

Measuring cups and
   spoons
Medium mixing bowl
Electric mixer
Rubber spatula

▸▸ Ingredients

2 cups confectioners'
   sugar
1 tablespoon unsalted
   butter
2 teaspoons light corn
   syrup
2½ tablespoons hot
   water, or more if needed

1 Put the confectioners' sugar, butter, corn syrup, and 2½ tablespoons water in the medium mixing bowl. With the electric mixer set on medium speed, beat until the mixture is well blended. The icing should be soft enough to go through a piping-bag tip. If it's not, add more hot water, a few drops at a time, and beat it in.
Use immediately.

Makes about 1 cup

HOW TO USE A PIPING BAG

Using a piping bag to decorate cookies is fun and easy. To write neat letters, practice first on a piece of waxed paper.

How to Fill

Choose a bag that will hold the amount of icing you need without being too big. Fit a decorating tip into the narrow end of the bag.
Twist the piping bag closed just above the tip to keep the icing from coming out while you fill the bag. Fold a cuff in the top of the piping bag and hold it in one hand. With a rubber spatula, put the icing in the piping bag. Unfold the cuff and twist the top of the bag closed. The bag should feel firm and full.

How to Pipe

Squeeze the piping bag with one hand to press out the icing. For neatness, guide the bag with the fingers of your other hand as you go.

Iced Buttery Cutouts

MAKES ABOUT 40

Clear a work space, then gather together the following equipment and ingredients:

▶▶ Equipment

Measuring cups and spoons
Mixing bowls
Wooden spoon
Electric mixer
Plastic wrap or aluminum foil
Baking sheets
Rolling pin
Cookie cutters of any shape
Metal spatula
Hot pads
Cooling racks
Pot holders
Icing spatula

▶▶ Ingredients

1½ cups all-purpose flour
1 teaspoon baking powder
¼ teaspoon salt
½ cup unsalted butter, softened
¾ cup granulated sugar
1 egg
1½ teaspoons vanilla extract
Shortening for greasing baking sheets
Flour for rolling out dough
Rich and Creamy Icing (*recipe on page 18*)
Colored crystal sugars, candies, nuts, or whatever you might like for decorating

1 Put the flour, baking powder, and salt in a medium mixing bowl. Stir with the wooden spoon to mix the ingredients. Set the bowl aside.

2 Put the butter and sugar in a large mixing bowl. With the electric mixer set on medium-high speed, beat until the mixture is well blended. Add the egg and vanilla and beat until light and fluffy. With the electric mixer set on low speed, gradually add the flour mixture and beat until smooth.

3 Using your hands, gather the dough together into one big mass. Divide the dough mass in half. Roll each half into a ball. Pat the top of the ball to flatten it into a thick circle. Wrap each circle in plastic wrap or foil. Place them in the refrigerator to chill until firm enough to roll out, about 1 hour.

4 Adjust 2 oven racks to be in the center of your oven. Turn the oven on to 350°F. Lightly grease the baking sheets with the shortening.

5 With your fingers, sprinkle a light coating of flour over a flat work surface and the rolling pin. Remove 1 piece of dough from the refrigerator. Unwrap the dough and place it on the floured work surface. With the rolling pin, roll out the dough into a large circle about ⅛ inch thick.

6 Holding a cookie cutter firmly, press it straight down into the dough to cut out a shape. Lift the cutter carefully so you don't damage the shape. Repeat, cutting as close as possible to the previous shape, until you have cut out as many as you can.

GO TO NEXT PAGE ▶▶

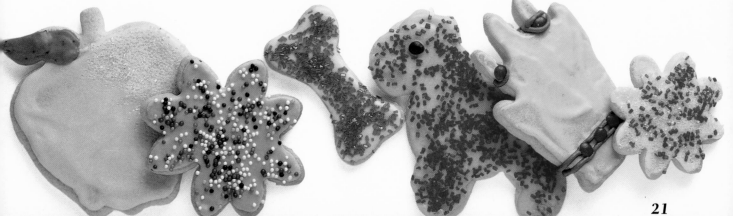

7 Gently slip the metal spatula under a few cutouts and lift them a little. Pull away the scraps of dough from around the shapes and set the scraps aside. Transfer the shapes to the greased baking sheets, spacing them about 1 inch apart.

8 Roll out and cut out the second piece of dough in exactly the same way. Transfer the shapes to the baking sheets.

9 Gather the scraps of leftover dough together into a ball and roll it out as before. Cut out more shapes and transfer them to the sheets.

10 Place the baking sheets in the preheated 350°F oven. Bake until the cookies are a light golden brown around the edges, 10 to 12 minutes.

11 Put the hot pads and cooling racks on your counter. Using the pot holders, remove the baking sheets from the oven and put them on the hot pads. Carefully slip the metal spatula under each cookie and transfer it to a rack. Let the cookies cool completely.

12 When the cookies are cool, make the Rich and Creamy Icing. Using the icing spatula, spread the icing on the cookies. Decorate the cookies while the icing is still soft so the colored sugars, candies, or nuts stay in place.

Gingerbread Pals

MAKES ABOUT 12

Clear a work space, then gather together the following equipment and ingredients:

▸▸ Equipment

Measuring cups and spoons
Baking sheets
Medium mixing bowl
Wooden spoon
Large mixing bowl
Electric mixer
Rolling pin
Cookie cutters of any shape
Metal spatula
Hot pads
Cooling racks
Pot holders
Piping bag and tips

▸▸ Ingredients

Shortening for greasing baking
 sheets
1½ cups all-purpose flour
2 teaspoons baking powder
1 teaspoon ground cinnamon
½ teaspoon ground ginger
¼ teaspoon ground cloves
¼ teaspoon salt
¾ cup firmly packed dark
 brown sugar
½ cup unsalted butter,
 softened
About 1½ tablespoons milk
Flour for rolling out dough
Decorating Icing (recipe on
 page 19)

1 Adjust 2 oven racks to be in the center of your oven. Turn the oven on to 375°F. Lightly grease the baking sheets with the shortening. Set the baking sheets aside.

2 Put the flour, baking powder, cinnamon, ginger, cloves, and salt in the medium mixing bowl. Stir with the wooden spoon to mix the ingredients. Set the bowl aside.

3 Put the brown sugar and butter in the large mixing bowl. With the electric mixer set on medium-high speed, beat until the mixture is well blended. Add the milk and beat until blended. Turn the mixer to low speed and gradually add the flour mixture. When the dough becomes too stiff for the beaters to work, turn the mixer off and use your fingers to scrape off all the dough from the beaters.

4 Add any remaining flour mixture to the bowl. Knead the mixture to mix in all the flour with a pressing and pushing motion. Continue kneading until the dough is smooth and well blended. Divide the dough in half. Roll each half into a ball.

5 With your fingers, sprinkle a light coating of flour over a flat work surface and the rolling pin. Place 1 ball of dough on the floured work surface. Roll out the dough into a large rectangle ⅛ to ¼ inch thick.

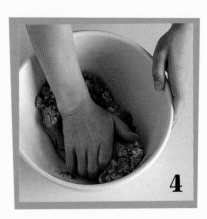

6 Holding a cookie cutter firmly, press it straight down into the dough to cut out a shape. Lift the cutter carefully so you don't damage the shape. Repeat, cutting as close as possible to the previous shape, until you have cut out as many as you can.

7 Gently slip the spatula under a shape and transfer it to a greased baking sheet. Repeat until all the shapes are on a baking sheet.

8 Roll out and cut out the second ball of dough. Transfer the shapes to the greased baking sheets.

9 Gather the scraps of leftover dough together into a ball and knead until smooth (if the dough becomes too crumbly to knead, add a few drops of milk). Roll out and cut out more shapes. Transfer them to the sheets.

10 Place the baking sheets in the preheated 375°F oven. Bake until the cookies are lightly browned and set, about 10 minutes.

11 Put the hot pads and cooling racks on your counter. Using the pot holders, remove the baking sheets from the oven and put them on the hot pads. Let the cookies cool for 2 minutes. Carefully slip the spatula under each cookie and transfer it to a rack. Let the cookies cool completely.

12 When the cookies are cool, make the Decorating Icing and decorate 🖌 the cookies as you like.

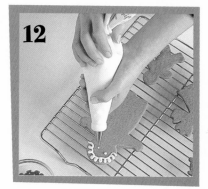

Sugar Stars

Clear a work space, then gather together the following equipment and ingredients:

▶▶ **Equipment**

Measuring cups and spoons
Medium mixing bowl
Wooden spoon
Rolling pin
Star-shaped cookie cutters
Metal spatula
Baking sheets
Small bowl
Pastry brush
Hot pads
Cooling racks
Pot holders

▶▶ **Ingredients**

1¼ cups all-purpose flour
5 tablespoons granulated sugar
½ cup unsalted butter, softened
Flour for rolling out dough
About 1 tablespoon milk
Colored crystal sugars for
　decorating

1 Adjust 2 oven racks to be in the center of your oven. Turn the oven on to 325°F.

2 Put the flour and sugar in the mixing bowl. Stir with the wooden spoon. Add the butter. With your hands, squeeze the ingredients together until they form a well-blended dough. Form the dough into a ball.

3 With your fingers, sprinkle a little flour over a work surface and the rolling pin. Place the ball of dough on the floured surface. Roll out the dough into a large circle about ¼ inch thick.

4 Holding a cookie cutter firmly, press it straight down into the dough to cut out a star. Lift the cutter carefully and repeat, always cutting as close as possible to the previous star, until you have cut out as many as you can.

5 Gently slip the spatula under a few stars and lift them a little. Pull away the dough scraps and set them aside. Transfer the stars to an ungreased baking sheet, spacing them ½ inch apart.

6 Gather the scraps of leftover dough together into a ball. Roll out and cut out more stars. Transfer them to the other baking sheet.

7 Put the milk in the small bowl. Dip the pastry brush in the milk and brush a light coating of milk over the top of each star. With your fingers, lightly sprinkle the stars with colored sugars.

8 Place the baking sheets in the preheated 325°F oven. Bake until the stars just begin to turn a pale golden brown, about 20 minutes.

9 Put the hot pads and cooling racks on your counter. Using the pot holders, remove the baking sheets from the oven and put them on the hot pads. Carefully slip the spatula under each star and transfer it to a rack. Let the cookies cool completely.

26

Happy Face Cookies

Clear a work space, then gather together the following equipment and ingredients:

▶▶ Equipment

Measuring cups and spoons
Mixing bowls
Wooden spoon
Electric mixer
Dinner plate
Waxed paper
Rolling pin
Cutting board
Plate, about 5 inches in diameter
Small, sharp knife
Baking sheets
Garlic press (optional)
Hot pads
Cooling racks
Pot holders
Metal spatula

▶▶ Ingredients

2 cups all-purpose flour
½ teaspoon baking powder
½ teaspoon salt
⅛ teaspoon baking soda
10 tablespoons unsalted butter, softened
½ cup firmly packed light brown sugar
¼ cup granulated sugar
1 egg
1 teaspoon vanilla extract
1 tablespoon unsweetened cocoa powder

1 Put the flour, baking powder, salt, and baking soda in a medium mixing bowl. Stir with the spoon to mix the ingredients. Set the bowl aside.

2 Put the butter, brown sugar, and granulated sugar in a large mixing bowl. With the electric mixer set on medium-high speed, beat until the mixture is light and fluffy. Add the egg and vanilla and beat until well blended. With the electric mixer set on low speed, add the flour mixture and beat to form a smooth dough.

3 Divide the dough in half and put one-half on the dinner plate. Set the plate aside. Add the cocoa to the dough remaining in the mixing bowl. With the electric mixer set on low speed, beat the dough until the cocoa is evenly blended into it.

4 Divide the cocoa-flavored dough in half. Use your hands to form each half into a ball. Divide the dough on the plate—the vanilla-flavored dough—in half, and form each half into a ball.

5 Tear off a large sheet of waxed paper, put it on a work surface, and put 1 dough ball on top. Cover with a second sheet of waxed paper. With the rolling pin, roll out the dough (between the sheets of waxed paper) into a circle about ⅛ inch thick. Place the rolled-out dough (still between the sheets of waxed paper) in the refrigerator to chill until firm, about 10 minutes. Roll out the remaining 3 balls in exactly the same way and refrigerate until firm.

6 Adjust 2 oven racks to be in the center of your oven. Turn the oven on to 350°F.

7

7 Remove 1 dough circle from the refrigerator and place it on the cutting board. Peel off the top sheet of waxed paper. Using the 5-inch plate as a guide, cut out a circle ✒ from the center of the dough circle with the small knife. Pull away the dough from around the small circle and set the scraps aside. Transfer the small circle (the base of your cookie face) to an ungreased baking sheet by lifting the waxed paper and turning it upside down onto the baking sheet. Peel off the waxed paper. Repeat this step with the 3 dough circles still in the refrigerator, putting 2 dough circles on each baking sheet.

8 With the dough scraps, make a face 🖎 on each circle. Use the chocolate dough to make the faces on the vanilla circles, and the vanilla dough to make the faces on the chocolate circles. Push scraps of dough through the garlic press to make hair.

9 Place the baking sheets in the preheated 350°F oven. Bake until the cookies are a light golden brown around the edges, 10 to 12 minutes.

10 Put the hot pads and cooling racks on your counter. Using the pot holders, remove the baking sheets from the oven and put them on the hot pads. Let the cookies cool for 1 minute. Carefully slip the spatula under each cookie and transfer it to a rack. Let the cookies cool completely.

MAKES 32

Clear a work space, then gather together the following equipment and ingredients:

▶▶ Equipment 🥤

Measuring cups and spoons
Large mixing bowl
Electric mixer
Plastic wrap
Baking sheets
Parchment paper
Rolling pin
Icing spatula
Table knife
Waxed paper
Cooling racks
Hot pads
Pot holders
Metal spatula
Small sieve
Small spoon

5

Rugelach

▶▶ Ingredients 🥛

½ cup unsalted butter, softened
3 ounces cream cheese, softened
1 teaspoon granulated sugar
1⅓ cups all-purpose flour
Flour for rolling out dough
1 tablespoon confectioners' sugar

For cinnamon filling:
2 tablespoons granulated sugar mixed with 2 teaspoons cinnamon
For apricot filling:
4 tablespoons apricot jam

1 Put the butter, cream cheese, and granulated sugar in the large mixing bowl. With the electric mixer set on medium-high speed, beat until the mixture is well combined. With the electric mixer set on low speed, add the flour and beat until the mixture forms small crumbs. Using your hands, knead the crumbs in the bowl until you form a smooth dough. Divide the dough into 4 pieces.

2 Roll each piece of dough into a ball. Place each ball on a separate sheet of plastic wrap. With your hands, flatten each ball into a thick circle, wrap, and refrigerate until firm, about 30 minutes.

3 Adjust 2 oven racks to be in the center of your oven. Turn the oven on to 350°F. Line the baking sheets with the parchment paper.

4 With your fingers, sprinkle a light coating of flour over a flat work surface and the rolling pin. Remove 1 piece of dough from the refrigerator. Unwrap the dough and place it on the floured work surface. With the rolling pin, roll out the dough into a circle ⅛ inch thick. If the dough is too firm to roll, let it sit at room temperature for about 10 minutes.

5 Sprinkle either one-fourth of the cinnamon-sugar mixture over the dough circle, 🖐 or spread 1 tablespoon apricot jam over the circle with the icing spatula. With the knife, cut the circle into 8 pie-shaped wedges. Starting at the wide end of each wedge, roll up each piece of dough 🖐 to the narrow pointed end. Place the cookies on the parchment-lined baking sheets, setting them point-side down.

6 Repeat rolling, filling, and cutting until all of the dough and filling has been used.

7 Place the baking sheets in the preheated 350°F oven. Bake until the cookies are a very light golden brown, 15 to 25 minutes.

8 Place 2 sheets of waxed paper on your counter. Put the cooling racks over the paper. Set the hot pads on your counter. Using the pot holders, transfer the sheets to the hot pads. Let cool for 5 minutes. Carefully slip the spatula under each cookie and transfer it to a rack. Let the cookies cool completely.

9 Put the confectioners' sugar in the small sieve. With the bottom of the spoon, press the sugar through the sieve over the tops of the cookies.

Honey Graham Crackers

MAKES 24

Clear a work space, then gather together the following equipment and ingredients:

▶▶ Equipment

Measuring cups and spoons
Medium mixing bowl
Wooden spoon
Large mixing bowl
Electric mixer
Plastic wrap
Rolling pin
Ruler
Small, sharp knife
Metal spatula
Baking sheets
Table fork
Hot pads
Cooling racks
Pot holders

▶▶ Ingredients

2 cups whole-wheat flour
1 cup all-purpose flour
1 teaspoon baking powder
1 teaspoon ground cinnamon
½ teaspoon baking soda
¼ teaspoon salt

¾ cup firmly packed dark brown sugar
½ cup unsalted butter, softened
⅓ cup honey
1 teaspoon vanilla extract
7 to 8 tablespoons milk
Flour for rolling out dough

1 Adjust 2 oven racks to be in the center of your oven. Turn the oven on to 350°F.

2 Put the whole-wheat flour, all-purpose flour, baking powder, cinnamon, baking soda, and salt in the medium mixing bowl. Stir with the wooden spoon to mix the ingredients. Set the bowl aside.

3 Put the brown sugar, butter, honey, and vanilla in the large mixing bowl. With the electric mixer set on medium-high speed, beat until the mixture is well blended and fluffy.

4 Add one-fourth of the flour mixture to the sugar mixture and beat on low speed until blended. Add 2 tablespoons of the milk and beat until blended. Beat in another one-fourth of the flour and another 2 tablespoons of the milk. Beat in half of the remaining flour and another 2 tablespoons milk. Then beat in all of remaining flour and another 1 tablespoon milk. If the dough seems too dry, beat in a little more milk. (If mixture is too stiff for your mixer to beat, knead the dough in the bowl with your hands until it is smooth.)

5 Divide the dough into 4 equal pieces. Roll each piece into a ball. Wrap 3 balls separately in plastic wrap and set them aside.

6 With your fingers, sprinkle a light coating of flour over a flat work surface and the rolling pin. Put the unwrapped ball of dough on the floured work surface. With the rolling pin, roll out the dough into a 15-by-5-inch rectangle. (Do not press hard when you roll or the dough will stick.)

7

7 With the sharp knife and the straight edge of the ruler, trim the edges of the rectangle so they are even. Cut the rectangle crosswise into 6 smaller rectangles, ✍ each measuring 5 by 2½ inches.

8 Very carefully slip the spatula under each small rectangle and transfer it to an ungreased baking sheet. With the knife, mark a line across the center of each rectangle, without cutting through the dough, dividing it into 2 equal squares. Using the tines of the fork, poke a pattern of holes ✍ into each square. Roll out and cut the remaining dough.

9 Place the baking sheets in the preheated 350°F oven. Bake until the crackers are beginning to brown around the edges, 13 to 15 minutes.

10 Put the hot pads and cooling racks on your counter. Using the pot holders, remove the baking sheets from the oven and put them on the hot pads. Carefully slip the spatula under each cracker and transfer it to a rack. Let the crackers cool completely.

Clear a work space, then gather together the following equipment and ingredients:

▶▶ Equipment

Measuring cups and spoons
• Large mixing bowl
Electric mixer
Plastic wrap
Baking sheets
Parchment paper
Rolling pin
3-inch round cookie cutter
   or glass
Hot pads
Cooling racks
Pot holders
Metal spatula

▶▶ Ingredients

½ cup unsalted butter, softened
6 tablespoons sugar
2 eggs
1 teaspoon vanilla extract
2 cups all-purpose flour
Flour for shaping and
   rolling out dough
About ½ cup poppy seed
   or prune filling, apricot
   preserves, or cherry pie
   filling

Hamantaschen

1 Put the butter and sugar in the large mixing bowl. With the electric mixer set on medium-high speed, beat until the mixture is well combined. Add the eggs and vanilla and beat until the mixture is well blended. With the electric mixer set on low speed, gradually add the flour and beat to form a smooth dough.

2 Dust your hands with flour. Gather the dough together into one big mass and divide it in half. Roll each half into a ball. Pat the top of each ball to flatten it into a thick circle. Wrap each circle with plastic wrap and refrigerate until firm, about 30 minutes.

3 Adjust 2 oven racks to be in the center of your oven. Turn the oven on to 350°F. Line the baking sheets with the parchment paper.

4 With your fingers, sprinkle a light coating of flour over a flat work surface and the rolling pin. Remove 1 piece of dough from the refrigerator. Unwrap the dough and place it on the floured work surface. With the rolling pin, roll out the dough ¼ inch thick.

5 Holding the cookie cutter firmly, press it straight down into the dough to cut out a circle. Lift the cutter carefully so you don't damage the circle. Repeat, cutting as close as possible to the previous circle, until you have cut out as many as you can.

6 Pull away the scraps of dough from around the circles. Gather the scraps together into a ball. Roll out and cut out more circles.

7 Spoon a heaping teaspoonful of the filling into the center of each circle. Moisten your finger with cool water and rub the water over the inside edge of each circle. Lift up the edges of each circle at 3 points and pinch together tightly, making a triangle and leaving some of the filling showing in the center. Using both hands, gently transfer the filled cookies to the parchment-lined baking sheets, spacing them 1 inch apart. Repeat rolling, cutting, filling, and shaping the remaining dough.

8 Place the baking sheets in the preheated 350°F oven. Bake until the cookies are a very light golden brown, 12 to 15 minutes.

9 Put the hot pads and cooling racks on your counter. Using the pot holders, remove the baking sheets from the oven and put them on the hot pads. Let the cookies cool for 1 to 2 minutes. Carefully slip the spatula under each cookie and transfer it to a rack. Let the cookies cool completely.

Cookie Greeting Cards

MAKES ABOUT 8

Clear a work space, then gather together the following equipment and ingredients:

▶▶ Equipment

Measuring cups and spoons
Medium mixing bowl
Wooden spoon
Large mixing bowl
Electric mixer
Waxed paper
Rolling pin
Ruler
Baking sheets
Hot pads
Cooling racks
Pot holders
Metal spatula
Icing spatula
Piping bag and tips

▶▶ Ingredients

2¾ cups all-purpose flour
¾ teaspoon ground ginger
½ teaspoon baking soda
½ teaspoon salt
½ teaspoon ground cinnamon
⅛ teaspoon ground cloves
1 cup unsalted butter, softened
½ cup firmly packed dark brown sugar
⅓ cup molasses
Decorating Icing (*recipe on page 19*)
Food coloring (optional)

1 Adjust 2 oven racks to be in the center of your oven. Turn the oven on to 375°F. Put the flour, ginger, baking soda, salt, cinnamon, and cloves in the medium mixing bowl. Stir with the wooden spoon.

2 Put the butter and brown sugar in the large mixing bowl. With the electric mixer set on medium-high speed, beat until well blended. Add the molasses and beat until smooth. With the electric mixer set on low speed, gradually add the flour mixture and beat until well blended. Using your hands, shape the dough into a ball.

3 Divide the dough into 6 pieces. Put 1 dough piece on a sheet of waxed paper. Cover with a second sheet of waxed paper. With the rolling pin, roll out the dough (between the sheets of waxed paper) ¼ inch thick. Peel off the top sheet of waxed paper. Measure the dough with a ruler and cut it into a 5-inch square. Gather the scraps from around the dough and set them aside to reroll and cut.

4 To transfer the dough square to the baking sheet, lift the waxed paper and turn it upside down onto an ungreased baking sheet. Carefully peel off ☜ the paper. (If the dough sticks to the paper, place it in the refrigerator for 10 minutes, then try again.) Repeat rolling, cutting, and transferring the remaining dough and scraps.

5 Place the baking sheets in the preheated 375°F oven. Bake until the cookies are a light golden brown, 8 to 10 minutes.

6 Put the hot pads and cooling racks on your counter. Using the pot holders, remove the baking sheets from the oven and

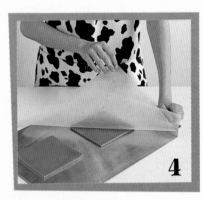

4

put them on the hot pads. Let the cookies cool for 1 to 2 minutes. Carefully slip the metal spatula under each cookie and transfer it to a rack. Let the cookies cool completely.

7 You can decorate the cookie cards in two ways: One way is to cover the surface of each cookie card with white icing and then write a message on the white icing with colored icing. To do this, make 1 recipe Decorating Icing. Spread the icing over the tops of the cookies with the icing spatula. Set aside until the icing sets. Make another batch of Decorating Icing and tint it one or several colors with a few drops of food coloring. Use the piping bag to write messages ☞ on the cookies (see directions on page 19). Set aside until the icing sets. The other way to decorate the cookies is to make 1 recipe Decorating Icing and use it to write messages on the cookie cards. (Do not store these cookies covered, as they will soften.)

37

Chocolate Chip Cookies

Clear a work space, then gather together the following equipment and ingredients:

▸▸ Equipment

Measuring cups and spoons
Baking sheets
Medium mixing bowl
Wooden spoon
Large mixing bowl
Electric mixer
Rubber spatula
Tablespoons
Hot pads
Cooling racks
Pot holders
Metal spatula

▸▸ Ingredients

Shortening for greasing baking
   sheets
1 cup plus 2 tablespoons
   all-purpose flour
½ teaspoon baking soda
¼ teaspoon salt
½ cup unsalted butter, softened
½ cup firmly packed dark
   brown sugar
⅓ cup granulated sugar
1 egg
1 teaspoon vanilla extract
1 cup semisweet chocolate chips

1 Adjust 2 oven racks to be in the center of your oven. Turn the oven on to 350°F. Generously grease the baking sheets with the shortening. Set the baking sheets aside.

2 Put the flour, baking soda, and salt in the medium mixing bowl. Stir with the wooden spoon to mix the ingredients. Set the bowl aside.

3 Put the butter, brown sugar, and granulated sugar in the large mixing bowl. With the electric mixer set on medium-high speed, beat until the mixture is well blended. Add the egg and vanilla and beat until the mixture is smooth and creamy. (As you beat, turn off the mixer occasionally and scrape down the sides of the bowl with the rubber spatula.) With the mixer set on low speed, gradually add the flour mixture and beat until blended. Stir in the chocolate chips.

4 Drop the dough by very rounded tablespoonfuls onto the greased baking sheets, spacing the mounds about 2 inches apart.

5 Place the baking sheets in the preheated 350°F oven. Bake until the cookies are nicely browned, 11 to 15 minutes.

6 Put the hot pads and cooling racks on your counter. Using the pot holders, remove the baking

sheets from the oven and put them on the hot pads. Let the cookies cool for 3 to 4 minutes. Carefully slip the spatula under each cookie and transfer it to a rack. Let the cookies cool completely.

MAKES ABOUT 48

Clear a work space, then gather together the following equipment and ingredients:

▶▶ Equipment

Measuring cups and spoons
Baking sheets
Cutting board and sharp knife
Medium mixing bowl
Wooden spoon
Large mixing bowl
Electric mixer
Teaspoons
Hot pads
Cooling rack
Pot holders
Metal spatula

Raisin Hermits

▶▶ Ingredients

Shortening for greasing baking sheets
¾ cup chopped nuts (walnuts are good)
1¾ cups all-purpose flour
1 teaspoon ground cinnamon
½ teaspoon baking soda
½ teaspoon ground nutmeg
¼ teaspoon salt
1 cup firmly packed dark brown sugar
½ cup unsalted butter, softened
¼ cup milk
1 egg
1 cup raisins

1 Adjust 2 oven racks to be in the center of your oven. Turn the oven on to 375°F. Lightly grease the baking sheets with the shortening. Set the baking sheets aside.

2 If the nuts are not already chopped, put them on the cutting board. With the sharp knife, chop coarsely (see page 14). Set aside.

3 Put the flour, cinnamon, baking soda, nutmeg, and salt in the medium mixing bowl. Stir with the wooden spoon to mix the ingredients. Set the bowl aside.

4 Put the brown sugar, butter, milk, and egg in the large mixing bowl. With the electric mixer set on medium-high speed, beat until the mixture is smooth and creamy. With the electric mixer speed set on low speed, gradually beat in the flour mixture to form a dough. Stir in the raisins and nuts.

5 Drop the dough by rounded teaspoonfuls onto the greased baking sheets, spacing the mounds 1 inch apart.

6 Place the baking sheets in the preheated 375°F oven. Bake until the cookies are lightly browned, 8 to 10 minutes.

7 Put the hot pads and cooling racks on your counter. Using the pot holders, remove the baking sheets from the oven and put them on the hot pads. Carefully slip the spatula under each cookie and transfer it to a rack. Let the cookies cool completely.

Lacy Oatmeal Crisps

MAKES ABOUT 40

Clear a work space, then gather together the following equipment and ingredients:

▸▸ Equipment

Measuring cups and spoons
Large mixing bowl
Electric mixer
Wooden spoon
Teaspoons
Baking sheets
Hot pads
Cooling racks
Pot holders
Metal spatula

▸▸ Ingredients

¾ cup firmly packed light
  brown sugar
½ cup unsalted butter, softened
2 tablespoons milk

1 teaspoon vanilla extract
¼ teaspoon salt
1¼ cups quick-cooking
  rolled oats
2 tablespoons all-purpose flour

1 Adjust 2 oven racks to be in the center of your oven. Turn the oven on to 350°F.

2 Put the brown sugar, butter, milk, vanilla, and salt in the large mixing bowl. With the electric mixer set on medium-high speed, beat until the mixture is well blended. Using the wooden spoon, stir in the oats and flour.

3 Drop the dough by level teaspoonfuls onto the ungreased baking sheets, spacing the mounds 2 inches apart (you need plenty of space around them because the cookies will spread during baking).

4 Place the baking sheets in the preheated 350°F oven. Bake until the cookies are a light golden brown around the edges, 8 to 12 minutes.

5 Put the hot pads and cooling racks on your counter. Using the pot holders, remove the baking sheets from the oven and put them on the hot pads. Let the cookies cool for about 2 minutes.

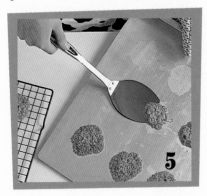

(Timing is important. If the cookies don't cool long enough, they will lose their shape. If they cool too long, they will stick to the baking sheets.) Carefully slip the spatula under each cookie and transfer it to a rack. Let the cookies cool completely.

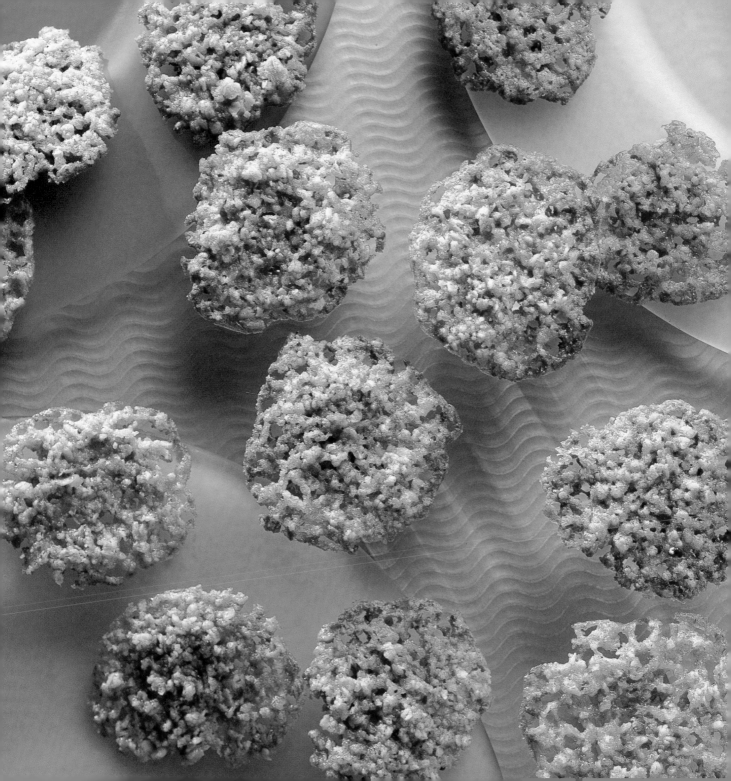

Date Dreams

Clear a work space, then gather together the following equipment and ingredients:

▶▶ Equipment

Measuring cups and spoons
Baking sheets
Medium mixing bowl
Wooden spoon
Large mixing bowl
Electric mixer
Rubber spatula
Teaspoons
Hot pads
Cooling racks
Pot holders
Metal spatula

▶▶ Ingredients

Shortening for greasing baking sheets
1¼ cups all-purpose flour
1 teaspoon ground cinnamon
½ teaspoon ground nutmeg
½ teaspoon baking soda
¼ teaspoon baking powder
Big pinch of salt

¾ cup firmly packed dark brown sugar
6 tablespoons unsalted butter, softened
1 egg
1 teaspoon vanilla extract
½ cup sour cream
¾ cup chopped dates
About 50 pecan halves (optional)

1 Adjust 2 oven racks to be in the center of your oven. Turn the oven on to 375°F. Lightly grease the baking sheets with the shortening. Set the baking sheets aside.

2 Put the flour, cinnamon, nutmeg, baking soda, baking powder, and salt in the medium mixing bowl. Stir with the wooden spoon to mix the ingredients. Set the bowl aside.

3 Put the sugar, butter, egg, and vanilla in the large mixing bowl. With the electric mixer set on medium speed, beat until the mixture is light and creamy. (As you beat, turn off the mixer occasionally and scrape down the sides of the bowl with the rubber spatula.) Beat in the sour cream. With the electric mixer set on low speed, gradually add the flour mixture and beat just until blended. Beat in the dates.

4 Drop the dough by rounded teaspoonfuls onto the greased baking sheets, spacing the mounds 1 inch apart. If you like, press a pecan half into the top of each dough mound.

5 Place the baking sheets in the preheated 375°F oven. Bake until the cookies are lightly browned, about 10 minutes.

6 Put the hot pads and cooling racks on your counter. Using the pot holders, remove the baking sheets from the oven and put them on the hot pads. Carefully slip the spatula under each cookie and transfer it to a rack. Let the cookies cool completely.

Orange Coconut Macaroons

Clear a work space, then gather together the following equipment and ingredients:

▸▸ Equipment

Measuring cups and spoons
Can opener
Baking sheets
Parchment paper
Box grater
Large mixing bowl
Wooden spoon
Tablespoons
Cooling racks
Pot holders

▸▸ Ingredients

1 orange
1 package (14 ounces) flaked coconut
1 can (14 ounces) sweetened condensed milk
2 teaspoons almond extract
1 teaspoon vanilla extract

1 Adjust 2 oven racks to be in the center of your oven. Turn the oven on to 350°F. Line the baking sheets with the parchment paper. Set the baking sheets aside.

2 On the small holes of the box grater, grate the zest from the orange. ☛ (Grate only the colored part of the peel; don't grate the white part, called the pith, as it is bitter.) You should have about 1 teaspoon zest. Put the grated zest in the large mixing bowl.

3 Add the coconut, sweetened condensed milk, almond extract, and vanilla extract to the orange zest. Using the wooden spoon, stir the ingredients until well mixed.

4 Drop the mixture by scant tablespoonfuls onto the parchment-lined baking sheets, spacing the mounds about 1 inch apart. If necessary, wet your fingers with cool water and gently shape and press each mound to make it neat.

5 Place the baking sheets in the preheated 350°F oven. Bake until the macaroons are lightly browned, 10 to 15 minutes.

6 Put the cooling racks on your counter. Using the pot holders, remove the baking sheets from the oven and put them on the racks. Let the macaroons cool completely.

7 With your fingers, carefully peel the macaroons from the paper.

Giant Lemon Crisps

Clear a work space, then gather together the following equipment and ingredients:

▶▶ Equipment

Measuring cups and spoons
Baking sheets
Medium mixing bowl
Electric mixer
Rubber spatula
Tablespoons
Icing spatula
Hot pads
Cooling racks
Pot holders
Metal spatula

▶▶ Ingredients

Shortening for greasing baking
   sheets
½ cup unsalted butter, softened
⅓ cup sugar
1 egg
1 teaspoon lemon extract (or
   use orange extract to make
   Giant Orange Crisps)
¾ cup all-purpose flour

1 Adjust 2 oven racks to be in the center of your oven. Turn the oven on to 375°F. Generously grease the baking sheets with the shortening. Set the baking sheets aside.

2 Put the butter and sugar in the medium mixing bowl. With the electric mixer set on medium-high speed, beat until the mixture is well blended. Add the egg and lemon extract and beat until the mixture is fluffy. (As you beat, turn off the mixer occasionally and scrape down the sides of the bowl with the rubber spatula.) With the electric mixer set on low speed, add the flour and beat until blended.

3 Drop a tablespoonful of the batter at one end of the greased baking sheet. Dip the blade of the icing spatula into cool water and spread the batter into a thin circle 3½ to 4 inches in diameter. Make another circle on the baking sheet, spacing it well apart from the first. Repeat this process 👉, using all the batter

and both baking sheets. (You may need to wait until the first batch of cookies is baked, then wash the baking sheets. Dry them well, grease them again, and use them to bake more cookies.)

4 Place the baking sheets in the preheated 375°F oven. Bake until the edges of the cookies are just beginning to brown, about 6 minutes.

5 Put the hot pads and cooling racks on your counter. Using the pot holders, remove the baking sheets from the oven and put them on the hot pads. Let the cookies cool for 1 minute. Carefully slip the metal spatula under each cookie and transfer it to a rack. Let the cookies cool completely, about 10 minutes.

Melt-in-Your-Mouth Meringues

MAKES ABOUT 24

Clear a work space, then gather together the following equipment and ingredients:

▶▶ Equipment

Measuring cups and spoons
Baking sheets
Parchment paper
Large mixing bowl
Electric mixer
Rubber spatula
Teaspoons
Cooling racks
Pot holders

▶▶ Note

If it's a rainy day, don't make this recipe. Meringues lose their crispness and become sticky when the weather is humid.

▶▶ Ingredients

2 egg whites, at room temperature
  (*see page 14*)
¼ teaspoon cream of tartar
Pinch of salt
½ cup sugar
½ teaspoon vanilla extract

1 Adjust 2 oven racks to be in the center of your oven. Turn the oven on to 225°F. Line 2 baking sheets with the parchment paper.

2 Put the egg whites in the large mixing bowl. (Be sure they are free of all yolk; whites with even a touch of yolk will not beat well.) With the electric mixer set on low speed, beat the whites just until they are foamy. Add the cream of tartar and salt to the whites. With the electric mixer set on high speed, beat the whites until they stand in soft peaks when you lift the beaters. To check the peaks, first turn the mixer off. Slowly raise the beaters from the bottom of the bowl. They should pull the whites into a peak. A soft peak will have a mountain shape, but the top will droop and bend over.

3 With the electric mixer set on high speed, very slowly beat in the sugar, 1 tablespoon at a time. Occasionally stop the mixer and scrape down the sides of the bowl with the rubber spatula. Continue beating until the whites stand in straight peaks (no droops) when you lift the beaters, about 10 minutes. When the whites form stiff peaks, add the vanilla. Beat just until blended.

4 Drop the mixture by heaping teaspoonfuls onto the parchment-lined baking sheets, spacing the mounds 1 inch apart.

5 Place the baking sheets in the preheated 225°F oven. Bake the meringues for 1 hour, then turn off the oven and let them sit in the still-warm oven for 30 minutes. The meringues will become crisp as they sit.

6 Put the cooling racks on your counter. Using the pot holders, remove the baking sheets from the oven and put them on the cooling racks. Let the meringues cool completely.

7 With your fingers, carefully peel the meringues from the paper.

MAKES 12

Clear a work space, then gather together the following equipment and ingredients:

▶▶ Equipment

Measuring cups and spoons
Baking sheets
Parchment paper
Large mixing bowl
Electric mixer
Rubber spatula
Large spoon
Icing spatula
12 popsicle sticks
Cooling racks
Pot holders

▶▶ Note

If it's a rainy day, don't make this recipe. Meringues lose their crispness and become sticky when the weather is humid.

Strawberry Cookie Pops

▶▶ Ingredients

3 egg whites, at room
   temperature (see page 14)
¼ teaspoon cream of tartar
Pinch of salt
¾ cup sugar
2 tablespoons strawberry jam
4 or 5 drops red food coloring
Colored sprinkles and tiny
   colorful candies for decorating

1 Adjust 2 oven racks to be in the center of your oven. Turn the oven on to 225°F. Line 2 baking sheets with the parchment paper. Set the baking sheets aside.

2 Put the egg whites in the large mixing bowl. (Be sure they are free of all yolk; whites with even a touch of yolk will not beat well.) With the electric mixer set on low speed, beat the egg whites just until they are foamy. Add the cream of tartar and salt to the whites. With the electric mixer set on high speed, beat the whites until they stand in soft peaks when you lift the beaters. To check the peaks, first turn the mixer off. Slowly raise the beaters from the bottom of the bowl. They should pull the whites into a peak. A soft peak will have a mountain shape, but the top will droop and bend over.

3 With the electric mixer set on high speed, very slowly beat in the sugar, 1 tablespoon at a time. Occasionally turn off the mixer and scrape down the sides of the bowl with the rubber spatula. Continue beating until the whites stand in straight peaks (no droops) when you lift the beaters, about 10 minutes. When the whites form stiff peaks, add the strawberry jam and food coloring. Beat just until blended.

4 Using the large spoon, drop 6 equal-sized mounds of the mixture onto each parchment-lined baking sheet, spacing them 3 inches apart. Using the icing spatula, spread each mound into a circle ½ inch thick and about 3 inches in diameter. Insert a popsicle stick in the side of each circle, gently pushing the stick well into the center.

5 Decorate the tops of the circles with sprinkles and candies.

6 Place the baking sheets in the preheated 225°F oven. Bake the pops for 2 hours. Now you have a choice: You can remove the pops from the oven and let them cool at room temperature, in which case they will be crisp on the outside and chewy on the inside. Or you can turn off the oven and let the pops sit in the still-warm oven for 30 minutes, in which case they will be crisp all the way through.

7 Put the cooling racks on your counter. Using pot holders, remove the baking sheets from the oven and put them on the racks. Let the pops cool completely.

8 With your fingers, carefully peel the pops from the paper.

MAKES 36

Clear a work space, then gather together the following equipment and ingredients:

▸▸ **Equipment**

Measuring cups and spoons
Can opener
Cutting board and sharp knife
9-by-13-inch baking dish
Cooling rack
Pot holders
Small, sharp knife
Metal spatula

▸▸ **Ingredients**

¾ cup chopped mixed dried
  fruits (choose a combination
  of raisins, dried apricots,
  dates, pears, and apples)
½ cup unsalted butter, cut into
  pieces
1½ cups graham cracker
  crumbs
1 can (14 ounces) sweetened
  condensed milk
1 cup semisweet chocolate chips
1 cup salted dry-roasted peanuts
1 cup flaked coconut

Good Gorp Bars

1 Adjust an oven rack to be in the center of your oven. Turn the oven on to 325°F.

2 If the fruits are not already chopped, put them on the cutting board. With the knife, chop into raisin-sized pieces (see page 14). Set the chopped fruit aside.

3 Put the butter in the 9-by-13-inch baking dish. Put the dish in your oven until the butter melts, about 5 minutes. As soon as the butter melts, put the cooling rack on your counter. Using the pot holders, remove the dish from the oven and put it on the rack. Let cool until just warm to touch, about 5 minutes.

4 Sprinkle the graham cracker crumbs in an even layer over the butter. Pour the sweetened condensed milk evenly over the crumbs. Sprinkle the chocolate chips evenly over the milk. Then add an even layer of peanuts, followed by the fruits, and finally the coconut. Using your hand, pat down on top of the  ingredients 🐾 to make everything even and compact.

5 Place the pan in the preheated 325°F oven. Bake until the top turns a light golden brown, 25 to 30 minutes.

6 Using the pot holders, remove the pan from the oven and transfer it to the rack. Let the cookie cool completely.

7 Run the sharp knife all the way around the inside edge of the dish to loosen the cookie from the sides of the dish. Make 5 equally spaced cuts the length of the dish, and then 5 equally spaced cuts the width of the dish, to make 36 bars. Using the metal spatula, remove the bars from the dish.

MAKES 16

Luscious Lemon Squares

Clear a work space, then gather together the following equipment and ingredients:

▶▶ Equipment

Measuring cups and spoons
Box grater
Cutting board and sharp knife
8-inch square cake pan
Cooling rack
Pot holders
Table fork
Medium mixing bowl
Electric mixer
Rubber spatula
Small sieve
Small spoon
Small, sharp knife
Metal spatula

▶▶ Ingredients

1 small lemon
7 tablespoons unsalted butter, softened
1 cup plus 2 tablespoons all-purpose flour
¼ cup plus 1 tablespoon confectioners' sugar
2 eggs
1 cup granulated sugar
½ teaspoon baking powder
Big pinch of salt

1 Adjust an oven rack to be in the center of your oven. Turn the oven on to 350°F. On the small holes of the box grater, grate the zest from the lemon (see page 15). Put the lemon on the cutting board. Using the sharp knife, cut the lemon in half crosswise. Squeeze enough juice from the lemon to measure 2 tablespoons. Set the zest and juice aside.

2 Put the butter in the 8-inch square cake pan. Put the pan in the oven until the butter melts, about 5 minutes. Put the cooling rack on your counter. Using the pot holders, transfer the pan to the rack. Let cool, about 5 minutes. Sprinkle the 1 cup flour and the ¼ cup confectioners' sugar over the melted butter. Using the fork, mix the ingredients to form a dough. Using your hand, press the dough evenly over the bottom of the pan. Return the pan to the oven. Bake the crust for 15 minutes.

3 Meanwhile, put the eggs and granulated sugar in the medium mixing bowl. With the electric mixer set on medium speed, beat until the mixture is well blended. With the mixer set on low speed, beat in the remaining 2 tablespoons flour, the lemon zest, the 2 tablespoons lemon juice, baking powder, and salt until well combined.

4 When the crust is done, using the pot holders, transfer the pan to the rack. With the rubber spatula, spread the topping over the hot crust. Return to the oven and bake until pale brown, 20 to 25 minutes.

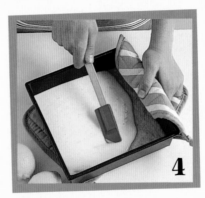

Using the pot holders, transfer the pan to the rack. Let cool.

5 Put the 1 tablespoon confectioners' sugar in the sieve. With the bottom of the spoon, press the sugar through the sieve over the top of the cookie. Using the sharp knife, cut into 16 squares. Using the metal spatula, remove the squares from the pan.

Clear a work space, then gather together the following equipment and ingredients:

▶▶ Equipment 🥄

Measuring cups and spoons
2 small bowls
Large mixing bowl
Electric mixer
10½-by-15½-inch baking pan
   with 1-inch sides
Table fork
Pastry brush
Hot pads
Cooling rack
Pot holders
Small, sharp knife
Metal spatula

Yummy Cookie Squares

▶▶ Ingredients 🥛

1 egg
1 cup unsalted butter, softened
1 cup plus 2 tablespoons sugar
1 teaspoon vanilla extract
2 cups all-purpose flour
1½ teaspoons ground cinnamon
½ cup chopped pecans

1 Adjust an oven rack to be in the center of your oven. Turn the oven on to 350°F.

2 Separate the egg (see page 14), putting the white in 1 small bowl and the yolk in another small bowl. Set both bowls aside.

3 Put the butter in a large mixing bowl. With the electric mixer set on medium-high speed, beat until the butter is smooth and fluffy. Slowly add the 1 cup sugar, continuing to beat until the mixture is well blended. Add the egg yolk and vanilla and beat until the mixture is light and fluffy. With the electric mixer set on low speed, beat in the flour and cinnamon to form a dough.

4 Put the dough in the ungreased 10½-by-15½-inch baking pan with 1-inch sides. Using your hand, pat the dough evenly over the bottom of the pan.

5 Using the fork, beat the egg white just until foamy. Using the pastry brush, brush the egg white evenly over the dough in the pan. Sprinkle the 2 tablespoons sugar and the pecans evenly over the dough.

6 Place the pan in the preheated 350°F oven and bake until light golden brown, about 30 minutes.

7 Put the hot pads and cooling rack on your counter. Using the pot holders, remove the pan from the oven and put it on the hot pad. Let cool slightly, about 10 minutes. Then, using the sharp knife, make 4 equally spaced cuts the length of the pan. 🔪 Then make 5 equally spaced cuts the width of the pan, to make 30 squares. (The cookies will be a bit gooey when you cut them, but will crisp as they cool.) Using the spatula, transfer the cookies to the rack. Let the cookies cool completely.

Double-Fudge Brownies

MAKES 16

Clear a work space, then gather together the following equipment and ingredients:

▸▸ Equipment

Measuring cups and spoons
9-inch square cake pan
Medium saucepan
Wooden spoon
Hot pad
Pot holders
Rubber spatula
Cooling rack
Small sieve
Small spoon
Sharp knife
Metal spatula

▸▸ Ingredients

Shortening for greasing cake pan
¾ cup granulated sugar
6 tablespoons unsalted butter
2 tablespoons milk
2 cups (about 12 ounces) semi-sweet chocolate chips
2 eggs
1 teaspoon vanilla extract
¾ cup all-purpose flour
¼ teaspoon baking soda
¼ teaspoon salt
2 tablespoons confectioners' sugar

1 Adjust an oven rack to be in the center of your oven. Turn the oven on to 325°F. Lightly grease the cake pan with the shortening.

2 Put the granulated sugar, butter, and milk in the medium saucepan. Set the pan on a burner of your stove and turn the heat on to low. Cook, stirring constantly with the wooden spoon, until the butter melts and the mixture just begins to boil, about 8 minutes. Turn off the heat. Put the hot pad on your counter. Using the pot holders, carefully put the saucepan on the hot pad. Add 1 cup of the chocolate chips to the mixture in the saucepan and stir with the wooden spoon until the chips melt. Let the mixture cool for 2 minutes.

3 Add the eggs and the vanilla to the mixture in the pan. Stir until all the ingredients are well mixed. Add the flour, baking soda, and salt. Stir until blended. Stir in the remaining 1 cup chocolate chips.

4 With the rubber spatula, scrape the mixture into the greased cake pan. Spread it evenly and smooth the top. Place the pan in the pre-heated 325°F oven. Bake until the brownies are set, 30 to 35 minutes.

5 Put the cooling rack on your counter. Using the pot holders, remove the pan from the oven and put it on the rack. Let the brownies cool completely.

6 When the brownies are cool, put the confectioners' sugar in the small sieve. With the bottom of the spoon, press the sugar through the sieve over the top of the brownies. Using the sharp knife, cut into 16 squares. Using the metal spatula, remove the brownies from the pan.

Chocolate, Marshmallow, and Peanut Butter Pizza

MAKES 1 PIZZA

Clear a work space, then gather together the following equipment and ingredients:

▶▶ Equipment

Measuring cups and spoons
12- or 14-inch pizza pan
Medium mixing bowl
Wooden spoon
Large mixing bowl
Electric mixer
Cooling rack
Pot holders
Pizza cutter or sharp knife

▶▶ Ingredients

Shortening for greasing pizza pan
1¼ cups all-purpose flour
¾ teaspoon baking soda
½ teaspoon baking powder
Big pinch of salt
½ cup unsalted butter, softened
½ cup creamy peanut butter
½ cup granulated sugar
½ cup firmly packed dark or light brown sugar
1 egg
Flour for shaping dough
½ cup salted dry-roasted peanuts
1½ cups miniature marshmallows
2 cups (about 12 ounces) semisweet chocolate chips

1 Adjust an oven rack to be in the center of your oven. Turn the oven on to 375°F. Grease the pizza pan with the shortening.

2 Put the flour, baking soda, baking powder, and salt in the medium mixing bowl. Stir with the wooden spoon. Set the bowl aside.

3 Put the butter, peanut butter, granulated sugar, brown sugar, and egg in the large mixing bowl. With the electric mixer set on medium-high speed, beat until the mixture is smooth and creamy. With the electric mixer set on low speed, add the flour mixture and beat just until blended.

4 Gather the dough into a rough ball and put it in the center of the greased pizza pan. Dust your hands with flour. With your hands, press the dough evenly over the bottom of the pan. With your fingers, pinch a little round rim around the edge of the circle.

5 Put the pan in the preheated 375°F oven. Bake until the crust is just beginning to brown, 8 to 12 minutes.

6 Put the cooling rack on your counter. Using the pot holders, remove the pan from the oven and put it on the rack. Carefully sprinkle the peanuts evenly over the crust. Sprinkle the marsh-

4

mallows evenly over the peanuts. Sprinkle the chocolate chips  evenly over the marshmallows. Using the pot holders, immediately return the pan to the oven. Bake until the marshmallows are puffy and lightly browned, 5 to 8 minutes.

7 Using the pot holders, remove the pan from the oven and put it on the rack. Let the pizza cool until the chocolate is firm, about 3 hours.

8 With the pizza cutter, cut the pizza in the pan into about 20 wedges.

Clear a work space, then gather together the following equipment and ingredients:

▸▸ Equipment

Measuring cups and spoons
9-inch square cake pan
Large mixing bowl
Wooden spoon
Electric mixer
Rubber spatula
Toothpick
Cooling rack
Pot holders
Medium mixing bowl
Icing spatula
Sharp knife
Metal spatula

6

Pumpkin Bites

▸▸ Ingredients

Vegetable oil to grease pan
1 cup all-purpose flour
¾ cup granulated sugar
1 teaspoon baking powder
1 teaspoon ground cinnamon
½ teaspoon ground allspice
¼ teaspoon salt
1 cup pumpkin purée
½ cup vegetable oil
2 eggs

For the cream cheese icing:
3 ounces cream cheese, softened
2 cups confectioners' sugar
1 teaspoon vanilla extract
1 to 2 tablespoons milk or
   cream

1 Adjust an oven rack to be in the center of your oven. Turn the oven on to 350°F. Lightly grease the 9-inch square cake pan with oil.

2 Put the flour, granulated sugar, baking powder, cinnamon, allspice, and salt in the large mixing bowl. Stir with the wooden spoon. Add the pumpkin, oil, and eggs. With the electric mixer set on medium speed, beat until the mixture is well blended. Using the rubber spatula, scrape the mixture into the oiled pan and spread it evenly.

3 Place the pan in the preheated 350°F oven. Bake the bars until a toothpick stuck into the center comes out clean (without uncooked batter on it), 18 to 25 minutes.

4 Put the cooling rack on your counter. Using the pot holders, remove the pan from the oven and put it on the rack. Let cool.

5 To make the icing: Put the cream cheese, confectioners' sugar, vanilla, and 1 tablespoon milk or cream in the medium mixing bowl. With the electric mixer set at medium speed, beat until the mixture is smooth and creamy. If necessary, add a little more milk or cream, just enough to make the icing spreadable.

6 Using the icing spatula, spread the icing over the top of the pumpkin bars. Using the sharp knife, cut into 9 squares. Then cut each square in half on the diagonal to make two triangles. Using the metal spatula, remove the triangles from the pan.

Happy Birthday Blondie

Clear a work space, then gather together the following equipment and ingredients:

▸▸ Equipment

Measuring cups and spoons
10-inch springform pan
Aluminum foil
Medium mixing bowl
Wooden spoon
Large mixing bowl
Electric mixer
Rubber spatula
Toothpick
Cooling rack
Pot holders
Table knife
Serving plate
Icing spatula
Candles
Piping bag and tip (optional)

▸▸ Ingredients

Shortening for greasing pan
1½ cups all-purpose flour
1¼ teaspoons baking powder
½ teaspoon salt
1 cup firmly packed dark brown sugar
½ cup granulated sugar
½ cup unsalted butter, softened
2 eggs
1 teaspoon vanilla extract
Decorating Icing (*recipe on page 19*)
Assorted colorful candies for decorating
Marshmallows for decorating (optional)
Food coloring (optional)

1 Adjust an oven rack to be in the center of your oven. Turn the oven on to 350°F. Wrap the bottom plate of the springform pan with aluminum foil. Snap the pan closed around the bottom plate. Grease the foil and the sides of the pan with the shortening.

2 Put the flour, baking powder, and salt in the medium mixing bowl. Stir with the wooden spoon to mix the ingredients. Set the bowl aside.

3 Put the brown sugar, granulated sugar, and butter in the large mixing bowl. With the electric mixer set on medium-high speed, beat until the mixture is well combined. Add the eggs and vanilla and beat until the mixture is light and creamy, turning off the mixer often to scrape down the sides of the bowl with the rubber spatula. With the electric mixer set on low speed, add the flour mixture and beat until well blended.

4 Scrape the batter into the greased pan. Spread it evenly and smooth the top with the rubber spatula.

5 Place the pan in the preheated 350°F oven. Bake until the top is a light golden brown and a toothpick ⟍ stuck into the center comes out clean (without uncooked batter on it), about 30 minutes.

6 Put the cooling rack on your counter. Using the pot holders, remove the pan from the oven and put it on the cooling rack. Let the blondie cool completely.

7 Run the knife along the inside edges of the pan to loosen the blondie from the pan sides. Release the clamp on the side of the pan and lift it away. Invert the blondie onto the cooling rack and remove the bottom of the pan. Then invert it again, so the blondie is right side up, onto the serving plate.

8 Make the Decorating Icing.

9 With the icing spatula, spread the icing over the cake. Quickly, before the icing has time to set, decorate the cake ☞ with candies. If you like, you can stick birthday candles into the large marshmallows and arrange them on the cake. Set the cake aside until the icing is set.

10 At this point, if you like, make another batch of Decorating Icing. Tint it a color by adding a few drops of food coloring and use it to write "Happy Birthday" on the cake with the piping bag and tip.

MAKES 20

Clear a work space, then gather together the following equipment and ingredients:

▶▶ Equipment

Measuring cups and spoons
9-by-13-inch baking dish
Large mixing bowl
Wooden spoon
Electric mixer
Rubber spatula
Cooling rack
Pot holders
Small, sharp knife
Metal spatula

2

Pecan Pie Bars

▶▶ Ingredients

Shortening for greasing dish

For the crust:

1⅓ cups all-purpose flour
½ cup firmly packed light
  brown sugar
½ teaspoon baking powder
½ cup unsalted butter cut into
  pieces, softened

For the topping:

¾ cup dark corn syrup
¼ cup firmly packed light
  brown sugar
3 tablespoons all-purpose flour
2 eggs
1 teaspoon vanilla extract
Big pinch of salt
1 cup chopped pecans

1 Adjust an oven rack to be in the center of your oven. Turn the oven on to 350°F. Lightly grease the 9-by-13-inch baking dish with the shortening. Set the dish aside.

2 To make the crust: Put the flour, sugar, and baking powder in the large mixing bowl. Stir with the wooden spoon to mix the ingredients. Put the butter on top of the flour mixture. Rub the ingredients together with your fingers until fine crumbs form. Press the crumbs evenly ✐ and firmly into the greased dish.

3 To make the topping: Put the corn syrup, sugar, flour, eggs, vanilla, and salt in the large mixing bowl. With the electric mixer set on medium speed, beat until the mixture is well combined. Stir in the pecans. Using the rubber spatula, scrape the mixture out of the bowl onto the crust in the dish. Spread the topping evenly.

4 Place the dish in the preheated 350°F oven. Bake until the top is a light golden brown, 20 to 25 minutes.

5 Put the cooling rack on your counter. Using the pot holders, remove the dish from the oven and put it on the rack. Let cool completely.

6 Using the sharp knife, make 4 equally spaced cuts the width of the dish. Then make 3 equally spaced cuts the length of the dish, to make 20 bars. Using the metal spatula, remove the bars from the dish.

MAKES 16

Granola Bites

Clear a work space, then gather together the following equipment and ingredients:

▸▸ Equipment

Measuring cups and spoons
8-inch square cake pan
Small bowl
Tablespoon
Plate
Table fork
Medium mixing bowl
Electric mixer
Wooden spoon
Rubber spatula
Toothpick
Cooling rack
Pot holders
Sharp knife
Metal spatula

▸▸ Ingredients

Vegetable oil for greasing cake pan
⅓ cup all-purpose flour
½ teaspoon baking soda
½ teaspoon ground cinnamon
1 ripe banana

2 tablespoons firmly packed dark brown sugar
2 tablespoons vegetable oil
2 tablespoons honey
1 egg white (*see page 14*)
1 teaspoon vanilla extract
1⅓ cups granola

1 Adjust an oven rack to be in the center of your oven. Turn the oven on to 350°F. Lightly grease the 8-inch square cake pan with oil. Set the pan aside.

2 Put the flour, baking soda, and cinnamon in the small bowl. Stir with the tablespoon to mix the ingredients. Set the bowl aside.

3 Peel the banana and set it on the plate. Mash the banana 🔪 with the fork. Put the banana in the medium mixing bowl. Add the brown sugar, oil, honey, egg white, and vanilla to the bowl. With the electric mixer set on medium speed, beat just until the mixture is blended. With the electric mixer set on low speed, beat in the flour mixture just until blended. With the wooden spoon, stir in the granola.

4 Using the rubber spatula, scrape the mixture into the oiled pan, then spread the mixture evenly in the pan.

5 Place the pan in the preheated 350°F oven. Bake until the top is a light golden brown and a toothpick stuck into the center comes out clean (without uncooked batter on it), about 15 minutes.

6 Put the cooling rack on your counter. Using the pot holders, remove the pan from the oven and put it on the rack. Let cool completely. Using the sharp knife, cut into 16 squares. Using the metal spatula, remove the bars from the pan.

3

Chocolate Nut Bark

MAKES ABOUT 34

Clear a work space, then gather together the following equipment and ingredients:

▶▶ Equipment

Measuring cups and spoons
Cutting board and sharp knife
Large mixing bowl
Electric mixer
10½-by-15½-inch baking pan
    with 1-inch sides
Rubber spatula
Hot pad
Pot holders
Cooling rack
Icing spatula

▶▶ Ingredients

1 cup chopped nuts (pecans
    or salted dry-roasted peanuts
    are good)
½ cup unsalted butter, softened
½ cup firmly packed dark or
    light brown sugar
1 egg yolk (*see page 14*)
1 teaspoon vanilla extract
1 cup all-purpose flour
2½ cups (about 15 ounces)
    semisweet chocolate chips

1 Adjust an oven rack to be in the center of your oven. Turn the oven on to 350°F.

2 If the nuts are not already chopped, put them on the cutting board. With the sharp knife, chop coarsely (see page 14). Set aside.

3 Put the butter, sugar, egg yolk, and vanilla in the large mixing bowl. With the electric mixer set on medium-high speed, beat until the mixture is well blended. With the electric mixer set on low speed, add the flour and beat until the mixture is blended.

4 Put the dough in the ungreased baking pan. With the rubber spatula or your fingers, spread the dough ☞ over the entire bottom of the pan to make a smooth, thin layer. (Don't leave holes in the dough and be sure the dough is even, not thin in some areas and thick in others. You may feel that you

don't have enough dough, but if you don't taste it, and you use the correct-size pan, you will have just enough to cover the bottom.)

5 Place the pan in the preheated 350°F oven. Bake until the dough is set, about 10 minutes.

6 Put the hot pad on your counter. Using the pot holders, remove the pan from the oven and put it on the hot pad. Immediately sprinkle the chocolate chips evenly over the dough.

7 Using the pot holders, immediately return the pan to the oven. Bake until the dough is a very light golden brown and the chocolate is melted, about 5 minutes. (The cookie should bake about 15 minutes in all; watch carefully so that it doesn't burn.)

8 Put the cooling rack on your counter. Using the pot holders, remove the pan from the oven and put it on the rack. With the icing spatula, immediately spread the melted chocolate over the entire top of the dough to form a smooth, even layer, using a pot holder to steady the pan if necessary. Carefully sprinkle the chopped nuts evenly over the chocolate. Let the cookie cool completely.

9 When the cookie is cool, put the pan in your freezer and let the chocolate harden. This will take about 20 minutes.

10 When the chocolate is hard, remove the pan from the freezer. Break the cookie 🖙 into irregularly shaped pieces.

MAKES 16

Rocky Roads

Clear a work space, then gather together the following equipment and ingredients:

▶▶ Equipment 🥘

Measuring cups and spoons
8-inch square cake pan
Cutting board and sharp knife
Large mixing bowl
Wooden spoon
Medium saucepan
Rubber spatula
Plastic wrap or aluminum foil
Metal spatula

▶▶ Ingredients 🥛

Unsalted butter for greasing pan
¼ cup chopped pecans
1½ cups graham cracker crumbs
1¼ cups miniature marshmallows
¾ cup confectioners' sugar
2 tablespoons plus ½ cup milk
2 cups (about 12 ounces)
   semisweet chocolate chips
3 tablespoons unsalted butter

1 Generously grease the 8-inch square cake pan with butter.

2 If the pecans are not already chopped, put them on the cutting board. With the sharp knife, chop coarsely (see page 14). Put the crumbs, marshmallows, ½ cup of the confectioners' sugar, pecans, and the 2 tablespoons milk in the large mixing bowl. Stir with the wooden spoon to mix the ingredients.

3 Put the remaining ½ cup milk, chocolate chips, and the 3 table-spoons butter in the medium saucepan. Set the saucepan on a burner of your stove and turn the heat on to low. Heat the mixture, stirring constantly with the wooden spoon, until the chocolate and butter melt and the mixture is smooth, about 4 minutes.

4 Pour half of the melted chocolate mixture (about ¾ cup) over the crumb mixture 🥄 (leave the second half in the saucepan). Stir the chocolate and crumb mixture until it is well blended. Spoon the mixture into the buttered pan. With your hand, press it evenly over the pan bottom.

5 Add the remaining ¼ cup confectioners' sugar to the melted chocolate mixture in the saucepan and stir until well mixed. Using the rubber spatula, scrape the chocolate from the saucepan onto the top of the mixture in the baking pan and spread it evenly. Cover loosely with plastic wrap or foil. Place the pan in the refrigerator until the chocolate is set, about 30 minutes.

6 Using the sharp knife, cut into 16 squares. Using the metal spatula, remove the squares from the pan.

4

MAKES ABOUT 24

Clear a work space, then gather together the following equipment and ingredients:

▶▶ Equipment

Measuring cups and spoons
Small bowl
Tablespoon
Medium mixing bowl
Large mixing bowl
Electric mixer
Baking sheets
Hot pads
Cooling racks
Pot holders
Metal spatula

4

Snickerdoodles

▶▶ Ingredients

2 tablespoons plus ¾ cup sugar
2 teaspoons ground cinnamon
1⅓ cups all-purpose flour
1 teaspoon cream of tartar
½ teaspoon baking soda
Big pinch of salt
½ cup unsalted butter, softened
1 egg
½ teaspoon vanilla extract

1 Adjust 2 oven racks to be in the center of your oven. Turn the oven on to 400°F.

2 Put the 2 tablespoons sugar and the cinnamon in the small bowl. Stir with the spoon until well mixed. Set the cinnamon-sugar mixture aside. Put the flour, cream of tartar, baking soda, and salt in the medium mixing bowl. Stir with the spoon to mix the ingredients. Set the flour mixture aside.

3 Put the butter, ¾ cup sugar, egg, and vanilla in the large mixing bowl. With the electric mixer set on medium-high speed, beat until the mixture is smooth and well blended. With the electric mixer set on low speed, add the flour mixture and beat until the ingredients are well combined.

4 Roll 1 rounded teaspoonful of the dough between your palms into a ball. Roll the ball in the cinnamon-sugar mixture. Put the sugar-coated ball on an ungreased baking sheet. Repeat with the remaining dough, spacing the balls 2 inches apart on the baking sheets.

5 Place the baking sheets in the preheated 400°F oven. Bake until the cookies are round, flat, and a light golden brown, 8 to 10 minutes.

6 Put the hot pads and cooling racks on your counter. Using the pot holders, remove the baking sheets from the oven and put them on the hot pads. Let the cookies cool for 1 to 2 minutes. Carefully slip the spatula under each cookie and transfer it to a rack. Let the cookies cool completely.

Jelly Thumbprints

Clear a work space, then gather together the following equipment and ingredients:

▶▶ Equipment

Measuring cups and spoons
Large mixing bowl
Electric mixer
Baking sheet
Small spoon
Hot pads
Cooling rack
Pot holders
Metal spatula

▶▶ Ingredients

½ cup unsalted butter, softened
3 tablespoons sugar
¾ teaspoon vanilla extract
Big pinch of salt
1 cup all-purpose flour
2 to 3 tablespoons jelly or preserves, any flavor

1 Adjust an oven rack to be in the center of your oven. Turn the oven on to 400°F.

2 Put the butter, sugar, vanilla, and salt in the large mixing bowl. With the electric mixer set on medium-high speed, beat until the mixture is light and fluffy. With the electric mixer set on low speed, add the flour and beat to form a smooth dough.

3 Roll rounded teaspoonfuls of the dough between your palms into balls. Place the balls on the ungreased baking sheet, spacing them about 1 inch apart.

4 With your thumb, make an indentation in the center of each ball. Using the small spoon, put some jelly or preserves into each indentation.

5 Place the baking sheet in the preheated 400°F oven. Bake until the cookies are just beginning to brown, about 10 minutes.

6 Put the hot pads and cooling rack on your counter. Using the pot holders, remove the baking sheet from the oven and put it on the hot pads. Let the cookies cool for 2 minutes. Carefully slip the spatula under each cookie and transfer it to the rack. Let the cookies cool completely.

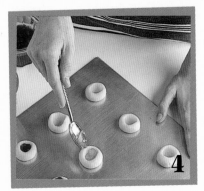

MAKES 24

Clear a work space, then gather together the following equipment and ingredients:

▶▶ Equipment

Measuring cups and spoons
Baking sheets
Cutting board and sharp knife
Mixing bowls
Wooden spoon
Electric mixer
Table fork
Hot pads
Cooling racks
Pot holders
Metal spatula

▶▶ Ingredients

Shortening for greasing baking
    sheets
¾ cup salted dry-roasted peanuts
1⅓ cups all-purpose flour
½ teaspoon baking powder
½ teaspoon baking soda
Big pinch of salt
½ cup unsalted butter, softened
½ cup crunchy peanut butter
½ cup granulated sugar
½ cup firmly packed dark
    brown sugar
1 egg
1 teaspoon vanilla extract

Double-Peanut Peanut Butter Cookies

1 Adjust 2 oven racks to be in the center of your oven. Turn the oven on to 375°F. Lightly grease the baking sheets with the shortening.

2 Put the peanuts on the cutting board. With the sharp knife, chop coarsely (see page 14). Set the peanuts aside.

3 Put the flour, baking powder, baking soda, and salt in a medium mixing bowl. Stir with the wooden spoon to mix the ingredients.

4 Put the butter, peanut butter, granulated sugar, brown sugar, egg, and vanilla in a large mixing bowl. With the electric mixer set on medium-high speed, beat until the mixture is smooth and creamy. With the electric mixer set on low speed, add the flour mixture and beat just until blended. Stir in the peanuts.

5 Roll rounded tablespoonfuls of the dough between your palms into balls. Put the balls on the greased baking sheets, spacing them 3 inches apart.

6 Flatten each ball by pressing on the top ☞ with the fork. (If the dough sticks to the fork, dip the fork into granulated sugar before pressing.) Each cookie should be about ½ inch thick.

7 Place the baking sheets in the preheated 375°F oven. Bake until the cookies are lightly browned, about 12 minutes.

8 Put the hot pads and cooling racks on your counter. Using the pot holders, remove the baking sheets from the oven and put them on the hot pads. Let the cookies cool for 2 minutes. Carefully slip the spatula under each cookie and transfer it to a rack. Let the cookies cool completely.

Clear a work space, then gather together the following equipment and ingredients:

▶▶ **Equipment**

Measuring cups and spoons
Mixing bowls
Wooden spoon
Electric mixer
Small bowl
Baking sheets
Hot pads
Cooling racks
Pot holders
Metal spatula

▶▶ **Ingredients**

1 cup all-purpose flour
1 cup quick-cooking rolled oats
½ teaspoon baking powder
½ teaspoon baking soda
¼ teaspoon ground cinnamon
¼ teaspoon salt
½ cup unsalted butter, softened
½ cup plus 2 tablespoons
    granulated sugar
½ cup firmly packed light
    brown sugar
1 egg
1 teaspoon vanilla extract

Old-fashioned Oatmeal Cookies

1 Adjust 2 oven racks to be in the center of your oven. Turn the oven on to 375°F.

2 Put the flour, oats, baking powder, baking soda, cinnamon, and salt in a medium mixing bowl. Stir with the wooden spoon to mix the ingredients. Set the bowl aside.

3 Put the butter, ½ cup granulated sugar, brown sugar, egg, and vanilla in a large mixing bowl. With the electric mixer set on medium-high speed, beat until smooth and creamy. With the electric mixer set on low speed, gradually beat in the flour mixture until blended.

4 Put 2 tablespoons granulated sugar in the small bowl. Roll 1 rounded tablespoonful of dough between your palms into a ball. Dip the top of the ball ☞ in the sugar and place the ball, sugar side up, on an ungreased baking sheet. Repeat with the remaining dough, spacing the balls 2 inches apart on the baking sheets.

5 Place the baking sheets in the preheated 375°F oven. Bake until the cookies are a light golden brown, 10 to 12 minutes.

6 Put the hot pads and cooling racks on your counter. Using the pot holders, remove the baking sheets from the oven and put them on the hot pads. Let the cookies cool for 2 minutes. Carefully slip the spatula under each cookie and transfer it to a rack. Let the cookies cool completely.

Chinese Almond Cookies

Clear a work space, then gather together the following equipment and ingredients:

▸▸ Equipment

Measuring cups and spoons
Baking sheets
2 small bowls
Electric blender
Medium mixing bowl
Wooden spoon
Large mixing bowl
Electric mixer
Table fork
Pastry brush
Hot pads
Cooling racks
Pot holders
Metal spatula

▸▸ Ingredients

Peanut oil for greasing baking
  sheets
1 egg
About 40 whole almonds
1 cup all-purpose flour
½ teaspoon baking powder
Big pinch of salt
½ cup unsalted butter, softened
½ cup sugar
1 teaspoon almond extract

1 Adjust 2 oven racks to be in the center of your oven. Turn the oven on to 350°F. Lightly grease the baking sheets with the oil.

2 Separate the egg (see page 14), putting the white in 1 small bowl and the yolk in another small bowl. Set both bowls aside.

3 Put 20 almonds in the container of the electric blender. Put the lid securely on the blender. Turn the blender on to high speed and blend the nuts until they are very finely chopped. Transfer the chopped nuts to the medium mixing bowl. Add the flour, baking powder, and salt. Stir with the wooden spoon. Set the bowl aside.

4 Put the butter and sugar in the large mixing bowl. With the electric mixer set on medium-high speed, beat until the mixture is well blended. Add the egg white and almond extract and beat until the mixture is smooth. With the electric mixer set on low speed, gradually beat in the flour mixture to form a dough.

5 Roll rounded tablespoonfuls of the dough between your palms into balls. Put the balls on the greased baking sheets, spacing them 2 inches apart. Using your fingers, lightly flatten each ball into a circle ⅓ inch thick.

6 Using the fork, beat the egg yolk until smooth. Using the pastry brush, brush the top of each dough circle 🖙 with the egg yolk. Place an almond in the center.

7 Place the baking sheets in the preheated 350°F oven. Bake until the cookies are a light golden brown, 12 to 16 minutes.

8 Put the hot pads and cooling racks on your counter. Using the pot holders, transfer the sheets to the hot pads. Let the cookies cool for 1 minute. Using the spatula, transfer the cookies to the racks. Let the cookies cool completely.

Snappy Ginger Cookies

MAKES ABOUT 22

Clear a work space, then gather together the following equipment and ingredients:

▶▶ Equipment

Measuring cups and spoons
Baking sheets
Small, sharp knife
Ginger grater or box grater
Small bowl
Tablespoon
Medium mixing bowl
Large mixing bowl
Electric mixer
Rubber spatula
Hot pads
Cooling racks
Pot holders
Metal spatula

2

▶▶ Ingredients

Shortening for greasing baking sheets
1 large chunk fresh ginger
3 tablespoons plus 1 cup sugar
1 teaspoon ground cinnamon
2 cups all-purpose flour
1½ teaspoons baking soda
1 teaspoon ground cloves
¼ teaspoon salt
⅓ cup unsalted butter, softened
⅓ cup shortening
1 egg
2 tablespoons dark corn syrup
¼ teaspoon vanilla extract

1 Adjust 2 oven racks to be in the center of your oven. Turn the oven on to 350°F. Lightly grease the baking sheets with the shortening.

2 Using the small, sharp knife, peel the skin from the ginger. Using the ginger grater, grate enough ginger to measure 2 teaspoons.

3 Put 3 tablespoons sugar and the cinnamon in the small bowl. Stir with the tablespoon until well mixed. Set the mixture aside.

4 Put the flour, baking soda, cloves, and salt in the medium mixing bowl. Stir with the spoon to mix the ingredients.

5 Put the butter and shortening in the large mixing bowl. With the electric mixer set on medium-high speed, beat until the mixture is smooth. Gradually add the 1 cup sugar and beat until the mixture is light and fluffy. Add the egg, corn syrup, vanilla, and grated ginger and beat until the mixture is very well blended. (As you beat, turn off the mixer occasionally and scrape down the sides of the bowl with the rubber spatula.) With the electric mixer set on low speed, gradually beat in the flour mixture to form a dough.

6 Roll 1 tablespoonful of the dough between your palms into a ball. Roll the ball in the cinnamon-sugar mixture. Put the sugar-coated ball on a greased baking sheet. Repeat with the remaining dough, spacing the balls 2 inches apart on the baking sheets.

7 Place the baking sheets in the preheated 350°F oven. Bake until the cookies are round, flat, and a light golden brown, 15 to 18 minutes.
8 Put the hot pads and cooling racks on your counter. Using the pot holders, remove the baking sheets from the oven and put them on the hot pads. Let the cookies cool for 1 to 2 minutes. Carefully slip the metal spatula under each cookie and transfer it to a rack. Let the cookies cool completely.

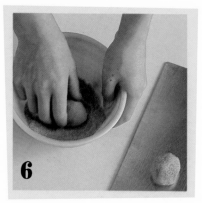

6

MAKES ABOUT 36

Clear a work space, then gather together the following equipment and ingredients:

▸▸ **Equipment**

Measuring cups and spoons
Cutting board and sharp knife
Large mixing bowl
Electric mixer
Baking sheets
Plastic wrap
Waxed paper
Cooling racks
Hot pads
Pot holders
Metal spatula
Small sieve
Small spoon

▸▸ **Ingredients**

½ cup finely chopped pecans
1 cup unsalted butter, softened
⅓ cup plus about ¼ cup
   confectioners' sugar
1 teaspoon vanilla extract
1¾ cups all-purpose flour

Snowballs

1 Adjust 2 oven racks to be in the center of your oven. Turn the oven on to 350°F.

2 If the pecans are not already chopped, put them on the cutting board. With the sharp knife, chop finely (see page 14). Put the butter, the ⅓ cup confectioners' sugar, and the vanilla in the large mixing bowl. With the electric mixer set on medium-high speed, beat until the mixture is smooth and creamy. With the electric mixer set on low speed, add the flour and beat just until the dough is blended and smooth. Beat in the pecans.

3 Roll 1 rounded teaspoonful of the dough between your palms into a ball and place on an ungreased baking sheet. (If the dough is too sticky to roll, cover the bowl with plastic wrap and place it in the refrigerator until the dough is firm, about 30 minutes.) Repeat with the remaining dough, spacing the balls 2 inches apart on the baking sheets.

4 Place the baking sheets in the preheated oven. Bake until the cookies are set and just starting to color around the edges, 15 to 18 minutes.

5 Place 2 sheets of waxed paper on your counter (it will catch the sugar topping and help in cleanup). Put the cooling racks over the waxed paper. Set the hot pads on your counter. Using the pot holders, remove the baking sheets from the oven and put them on the hot pads. Let the cookies cool for 1 to 2 minutes. Carefully slip the spatula under each cookie and transfer it to a rack.

6 Put the ¼ cup confectioners' sugar in the small sieve. With the bottom of the spoon, press the sugar ☞ through the sieve over the tops of the cookies. Let the cookies cool completely.

Sweethearts

MAKES ABOUT 20

Clear a work space, then gather together the following equipment and ingredients:

▶▶ Equipment

Measuring cups and spoons
Medium mixing bowl
Wooden spoon
Large mixing bowl
Electric mixer
Small bowl
Plastic wrap
Baking sheets
Hot pads
Cooling racks
Pot holders
Metal spatula

▶▶ Ingredients

2 cups all-purpose flour
¼ teaspoon baking powder
¾ cup unsalted butter, softened
¾ cup sugar
1 egg
1 teaspoon vanilla extract
Red food coloring
Flour for shaping dough

1 Adjust 2 oven racks to be in the center of your oven. Turn the oven on to 375°F. Put the flour and the baking powder in the medium mixing bowl. Stir with the wooden spoon to mix the ingredients.

2 Put the butter and sugar in the large mixing bowl. With the electric mixer set on medium-high speed, beat until the mixture is well combined. Add the egg and vanilla and beat until light and creamy. With the electric mixer set on low speed, add half of the flour mixture and beat until the mixture is blended. Beat in the remaining flour mixture until smooth. With your hands, gather the dough into a mass.

3 Divide the dough in half. Transfer one-half to the small bowl and cover with plastic wrap. Add a few drops of the red food coloring to the half remaining in the large bowl. With the electric mixer set on low speed, beat until the dough is evenly colored. Then keep beating in the food coloring, a few drops at a time, until the dough is the shade you desire. Cover the bowl with plastic wrap.

4 With your fingers, sprinkle a light coating of flour over a flat work surface. Roll 1 teaspoonful of the red dough between your palms into a ball. With your hands, roll the dough ball back and forth on the work surface to form a 6-inch-long rope. Put the dough rope on an ungreased baking sheet. Repeat rolling ropes with the remaining red dough and the white dough.

5 Place 1 red rope next to 1 white rope and press together gently. Twist the ropes together and form the twist into a heart shape, gently pinching the ends together. Repeat shaping hearts, spacing them about 1 inch apart on the baking sheets.

4

6 Place the baking sheets in the preheated 375°F oven. Bake until the cookies are firm and begin to turn a very light golden brown around the edges, 8 to 14 minutes.

7 Put the hot pads and cooling racks on your counter. Using the pot holders, remove the baking sheets from the oven and put them on the hot pads. Let the cookies cool for 2 minutes. Carefully slip the spatula under each cookie and transfer it to a rack. Let the cookies cool completely.

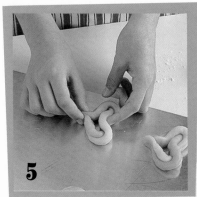

5

After-School Slice and Bakes

Clear a work space, then gather together the following equipment and ingredients:

▸▸ Equipment

Measuring cups and spoons
Medium mixing bowl
Wooden spoon
Large mixing bowl
Electric mixer
Plastic wrap
Cutting board and sharp knife
Baking sheets
Hot pads
Cooling racks
Pot holders
Metal spatula

▸▸ Ingredients

2 cups all-purpose flour
½ teaspoon baking soda
Big pinch of salt
1 cup sugar
½ cup unsalted butter, softened
1 egg
2 teaspoons vanilla extract
1 teaspoon milk
About ⅓ cup tiny colored sprinkles
Flour for shaping dough

1 Put the flour, baking soda, and salt in the medium mixing bowl. Stir with the wooden spoon to mix the ingredients. Set the bowl aside.

2 Put the sugar and butter in the large mixing bowl. Using the electric mixer set on medium-high speed, beat until well combined. Add the egg, vanilla, and milk and beat until light and creamy. With the electric mixer set on low speed, beat in the flour mixture and sprinkles to form a smooth dough. If the mixture is too stiff for your mixer to beat, knead the dough in the bowl with your hands until it is smooth. Gather the dough into a mass and then divide it in half.

3 Sprinkle a light coating of flour over a flat work surface. Using your hands, roll each piece of dough into a log 1½ inches in diameter and about 7 inches long. Flatten the ends. Wrap each log in plastic wrap and place in your freezer until firm enough to slice, about 30 minutes.

4 Adjust 2 oven racks to be in the center of your oven. Preheat the oven to 400°F. Remove 1 log from the freezer. Unwrap the log and place it on the cutting board. Using the sharp knife, cut the log into slices ¼ inch thick. (If the log is too hard to cut, let it sit at room temperature until it softens slightly.) Place the slices on the ungreased baking sheets, spacing them about 1 inch apart. Repeat with the second log (or keep it in the freezer to slice and bake another time).

5 Place the baking sheets in the preheated 400°F oven. Bake until the cookies are a very light golden brown, 8 to 10 minutes.

6 Put the hot pads and cooling racks on your counter. Using the pot holders, transfer the sheets to the hot pads. Using the spatula, transfer the cookies to the racks. Let the cookies cool completely.

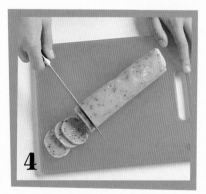

4

Beautiful Colorful Cookies

MAKES ABOUT 32

Clear a work space, then gather together the following equipment and ingredients:

▸▸ Equipment

Measuring cups and spoons
Large mixing bowl
Electric mixer
4 small bowls
4 table forks
Cutting board and sharp knife
Baking sheets
Hot pads
Cooling racks
Pot holders
Metal spatula

▸▸ Ingredients

½ cup unsalted butter, softened
½ cup confectioners' sugar
¾ teaspoon vanilla extract
1 cup all-purpose flour
Red, yellow, green, and blue
  food colorings

1 Adjust 2 oven racks to be in the center of your oven. Turn the oven on to 350°F.

2 Put the butter, confectioners' sugar, and vanilla in the large mixing bowl. With the electric mixer set on medium-high speed, beat until the mixture is creamy. With the electric mixer set on low speed, add the flour and beat to form a smooth and well blended dough.

3 Divide the dough into 4 equal pieces. Put each piece in a small bowl. Add a different color food coloring to the dough in each bowl. (Start with about 4 drops food coloring for each bowl, and add more if you want a deeper color.) Using a separate fork for each color, work the coloring into the dough until evenly blended.

4 Divide each piece of colored dough in half. Roll each half between your palms into a ball. You should have 8 balls: 2 red, 2 yellow, 2 green, and 2 blue.

5 First press the balls together and then roll them into a log 8 inches long. You are going to slice the log crosswise into thin circles, and you'll want each circle to have as many colors as possible. To achieve this, alternate the colors as you press the balls together.

6 Put the dough log on the cutting board. Using the knife, cut the log into slices ¼ inch thick. (If the dough is too soft to slice, put it in the refrigerator until firm enough to cut, about 30 minutes.) Place the slices on the ungreased baking sheets, spacing them about 1 inch apart.

5

7 Put the baking sheets in the preheated 350°F oven. Bake until the cookies are set, about 10 minutes.

8 Put the hot pads and cooling racks on your counter. Using the pot holders, remove the baking sheets from the oven and put them on the hot pads. Let the cookies cool for 1 to 2 minutes. Carefully slip the spatula under each cookie and transfer it to a rack. Let the cookies cool completely.

6

Chocolate-Mint Slice and Bakes

MAKES ABOUT 22

Clear a work space, then gather together the following equipment and ingredients:

▶▶ Equipment

Measuring cups and spoons
Medium mixing bowl
Wooden spoon
Large mixing bowl
Electric mixer
Plastic wrap
Cutting board and sharp knife
Baking sheets
Table fork
Hot pads
Cooling racks
Pot holders
Metal spatula

▶▶ Ingredients

1⅔ cups all-purpose flour
⅓ cup unsweetened cocoa
    powder
½ teaspoon baking soda
Big pinch of salt
1 cup firmly packed dark
    brown sugar
½ cup unsalted butter, softened
1 egg
2 teaspoons mint extract
Flour for shaping dough
About 24 chocolate mint candies
    (use Andes or Junior Mints, or
    similar)

1 Put the flour, cocoa, baking soda, and salt in the medium mixing bowl. Stir with the wooden spoon to mix the ingredients.

2 Put the sugar and butter in the large mixing bowl. With the electric mixer set on medium-high speed, beat until the mixture is well combined. Add the egg and mint extract and beat until light and creamy. With the electric mixer set on low speed, beat in the flour mixture to form a smooth dough. If the mixture is too stiff for your mixer to beat, knead the dough in the bowl with your hands until it is smooth.

3 Sprinkle a light coating of flour over a flat work surface. Dust your hands with flour, then gather the dough together into a mass and put it on the floured surface. Roll the dough into a log 2 inches in diameter and about 7 inches long. Wrap the log in plastic wrap and place in the freezer until firm enough to slice, about 30 minutes. (The log can stay in the freezer for several days.)

4 Adjust 2 oven racks to be in the center of your oven. Preheat the oven to 400°F. Remove the log from the freezer. Unwrap the log and place it on the cutting board. Using the sharp knife, cut the log into slices ⅛ inch thick. (If log is too hard to cut, let it sit at room temperature until it softens slightly.)

5 Place half of the slices on the ungreased baking sheets, spacing them about 1 inch apart. Put a chocolate mint in the center of each slice. Top the mint with another slice 🤏 of dough, making a sandwich.

5

6 With the tines of the fork, press the edges of ☞ each sandwich together, pressing all the way around each sandwich.

7 Place the baking sheets in the preheated 400°F oven. Bake until the cookies are set, 9 to 12 minutes.

8 Put the hot pads and cooling racks on your counter. Using the pot holders, remove the baking sheets from the oven and transfer them to the hot pads. Let the cookies cool for 1 to 2 minutes. Carefully slip the spatula under each cookie and transfer it to a rack. Let the cookies cool completely.

6

MAKES 1

Clear a work space, then gather together the following equipment and ingredients:

▸▸ Equipment

Paper plate, napkin, or paper
   towel, or microwave-safe plate
Long wood-handled fork
   or long, clean stick, freshly
   broken from a tree

▸▸ Ingredients

2 graham cracker squares
   (*store-bought or made from*
   the recipe on page 32)
⅓ to ½ chocolate candy bar
   (choose milk chocolate or
   semisweet chocolate; you
   need enough to cover
   1 graham cracker square)
1 large marshmallow

S'mores

CAMPFIRE OR FIREPLACE S'MORE

(Make this version only if an adult is on hand to supervise.)

1 Put 1 graham cracker square on the paper plate, napkin, or paper towel. Put the chocolate on top of the square; set aside.

2 Put the marshmallow on the end of the long wood-handled fork or long stick. Carefully hold the marshmallow over a low fire (campfire or fireplace), turning the fork or stick until the marshmallow turns golden brown, about 2 minutes.

3 Hold the toasted marshmallow on top of the chocolate-covered square. Using the second square, push the marshmallow off the fork or stick, then lay the second square on top ☞, forming a sandwich. Press the sandwich together gently. Eat while the s'more is hot.

MICROWAVE S'MORE

1 Put 1 graham cracker square on a paper plate, napkin, or paper towel, or microwave-safe plate. Put the chocolate on top of the square. Put the marshmallow on top of the chocolate.

2 Place in a microwave oven and microwave on HIGH until the marshmallow is puffy, 10 to 20 seconds.

3 Remove from the oven and top with the second graham cracker square, forming a sandwich. Press the sandwich together gently. Eat while the s'more is hot.

Marshmallow Surprises

Clear a work space, then gather together the following equipment and ingredients:

▶▶ Equipment

Measuring cups and spoons
3- to 3½-quart saucepan
Wooden spoon
Hot pad
Plate
Cellophane and ribbon
    (optional)

▶▶ Ingredients

¼ cup unsalted butter
About 30 large marshmallows
2 tablespoons creamy peanut
    butter
3 cups toasted rice cereal
⅓ cup salted dry-roasted
    peanuts

1 Put the butter in the saucepan. Set the saucepan on a burner of your stove and turn the heat on to low. Let the butter melt, about 2 minutes. Add 24 of the marshmallows. With the wooden spoon, stir until the marshmallows melt completely, about 5 minutes. Turn off the heat. Put the hot pad on your kitchen counter and set the pan on the hot pad.

2 Add the peanut butter to the melted marshmallows and stir well. Stir in the rice cereal and peanuts.

3 When the rice cereal mixture is cool enough to handle but still warm enough to mold, wet your hands with cold water. Gather about ½ cup of the mixture in one hand. Top with a marshmallow. Mold the cereal mixture ☛ around the marshmallow, making a compact ball. Set the ball on a plate.

4 Repeat with the remaining cereal mixture and marshmallows until they are used up. If you like, after the balls have completely cooled, wrap each ball in cellophane and tie with a ribbon.

Clear a work space, then gather together the following equipment and ingredients:

▶▶ **Equipment**

Measuring cups and spoons
Medium mixing bowl
Baking sheet
Table fork
Hot pads
Cooling rack
Pot holders
Sharp knife
Metal spatula

▶▶ **Ingredients**

1 cup all-purpose flour
½ cup unsalted butter, softened
¼ cup firmly packed light
   brown sugar
¼ teaspoon ground cinnamon

Shortbread

1 Adjust an oven rack to be in the center of your oven. Turn the oven on to 350°F.

2 Put the flour, butter, brown sugar, and cinnamon in the medium mixing bowl. With your hands, squeeze the ingredients together until the dough is smooth and well blended.

3 Put the dough in the center of the ungreased baking sheet. Using your fingers, pat the dough into a circle 6 to 6½ inches in diameter. Prick a design on top of the dough circle with the fork. Pinch the edges of the dough circle into a fancy pattern.

4 Place the baking sheet in the preheated 350°F oven. Bake until the shortbread is set and a light golden brown, about 25 minutes.

5 Put the hot pads and cooling rack on your counter. Using the pot holders, remove the pan from the oven and put it on the hot pads. Let the shortbread cool for about 8 minutes. Then, using the sharp knife, carefully cut the shortbread into 12 equal wedges. Carefully slip the spatula under each wedge and transfer it to the cooling rack. Let the shortbread cool completely.

Great Spritz

Clear a work space, then gather together the following equipment and ingredients:

▸▸ Equipment

Measuring cups and spoons
Large mixing bowl
Electric mixer
Small bowls (optional)
Cookie press and design plates
Baking sheets
Hot pads
Cooling racks
Pot holders
Metal spatula

▸▸ Ingredients

½ cup unsalted butter,
    softened
6 tablespoons granulated sugar
1 egg
½ teaspoon vanilla extract
¼ teaspoon almond extract
1¼ cups all-purpose flour
Food coloring, any color
    (optional)
Decorations such as candied
    cherries, colored sprinkles, or
    colored crystal sugars

1 Adjust 2 oven racks to be in the center of your oven. Turn the oven on to 400°F.

2 Put the butter, sugar, egg, vanilla, and almond extract in the large mixing bowl. With the electric mixer set on medium speed, beat until the mixture is smooth and creamy. With the electric mixer set on low speed, gradually add the flour and beat just until blended.

3 If you want to tint the cookies a color, add a few drops of food coloring to the dough and mix well with the electric mixer. If you want more than one color, divide the dough into pieces. Put each piece in a separate bowl and tint one piece at a time.

4 Attach the top and the handle to the cookie press (see page 17). Pack the dough into the tube. Fit a design plate into its holder and screw it onto the press. Holding the press up straight, push evenly on the handle to press out the dough into shapes onto the ungreased baking sheets. If you like, decorate the shapes with candied cherries (good on rosettes), colored sprinkles, or colored sugars.

5 Place the baking sheets in the preheated 400°F oven. Bake until the cookies are set and just starting to color around the edges, 7 to 10 minutes.

6 Put the hot pads and cooling racks on your counter. Using the pot holders, remove the baking sheets from the oven and put them on the hot pads. Let the cookies cool for 1 to 2 minutes. Carefully slip the spatula under each cookie and transfer it to a rack. Let the cookies cool completely.

Glossary

This alphabetical list gives you simple explanations for terms you'll find in this book and other cookbooks.

BAKE
To cook with hot, dry air in an oven.

BAKING POWDER
A powdered product that makes some doughs and batters rise during baking.

BAKING SODA
A white powder that, when combined with an acidic liquid such as buttermilk, produces carbon dioxide gas bubbles that make doughs and batters rise during baking.

BATCH
The quantity of food cooked or baked at one time, such as a batch of cookies.

BATTER
An uncooked mixture that is thin enough to pour, usually containing eggs, flour, and liquid.

BEAT
To mix ingredients vigorously, using a continuous circular motion.

BLEND
1. To combine two or more ingredients thoroughly. **Well blended** is used to describe ingredients that have been combined until no trace of any single ingredient is left.
2. To combine ingredients in an electric blender.

BUTTER, UNSALTED
Stores sell both salted and unsalted butter. Many recipes call for unsalted butter because it lets the cook control the amount of salt added.

CHILL
To place food in the refrigerator until cold.

CHOCOLATE
Made from the seeds ("beans") of the tropical cacao tree, chocolate is one of the world's favorite flavors. Bakers can buy chocolate in many different forms. The following kinds are used in this book: **Unsweetened cocoa powder** (different than hot cocoa mix) is a fine powder of pure chocolate liquor. **Semisweet chocolate** has sugar added, so it is a dark, sweet chocolate, sold as bars and chips. **Milk chocolate** is enriched with powdered milk, sold as bars.

CHOP
To cut ingredients such as nuts or dried fruit into pieces. **Coarsely chopped** means large pieces; **finely chopped** means small pieces.

COMBINE
To mix together two or more ingredients.

COOL (COMPLETELY)
To let something hot sit at room temperature until it is no longer warm to the touch, or until it has cooled completely to room temperature.

CREAM
The richest part of whole milk, cream is used to make doughs, batters, and icings extra rich and sometimes creamy. Depending on how much fat the cream contains, it is given a more specific name. The lightest, **half-and-half**, is a mixture made of equal parts milk and light cream. The richest, **heavy cream**, contains at least 36 percent fat, and is sometimes sold as **whipping cream** because you can whip it into soft or stiff peaks.

CROSSWISE
In the same direction as, or parallel to, a piece of food's or a pan's shortest side.

DOUGH
An uncooked mixture usually containing flour, liquid, and seasonings that is soft enough to be worked with your hands but is too stiff to pour.

DUST
To cover a food, hands, a work surface, or a tool very lightly with a powdery substance such as flour. Confectioners' sugar is often dusted onto the tops of cookies with a sieve.

EGGS
Sold in a range of sizes. Large eggs should be used for the recipes in this book. Eggs add moisture and richness to batters and doughs.

FAHRENHEIT (°F)
A temperature scale in which 32° (32 degrees) represents the point at which water freezes and 212° the point at which water boils. Oven temperature is indicated by °F.

FLOUR, ALL-PURPOSE
The most common kind of flour used in baking, blended from two kinds of wheat.

GRATE
To rub against a surface of small, sharp-edged rasps to make fine particles.

GREASE
To rub a surface of a baking sheet, pan, or dish with fat, such as butter, shortening, or oil, to keep cookies or other foods from sticking.

KNEAD
To work dough with your hands using a pressing, folding, turning motion. When dough is fully kneaded, it becomes smooth.

LENGTHWISE
In the same direction as, or parallel to, a piece of food's or a pan's longest side.

MEASURE
To place an ingredient in a measuring cup or measuring spoon to ensure an exact amount.

MELT
To heat a solid substance, such as butter or chocolate, until it becomes liquid.

PINCH
Amount of a dry ingredient that you can pick up between your thumb and forefinger.

PREHEAT
To heat the oven to a certain temperature before putting food in to cook. Preheat an oven for at least 15 minutes.

ROOM TEMPERATURE
The temperature of a comfortable room, not too hot or too cold. Butter is often brought to room temperature before it is combined with other ingredients, so it will soften slightly and blend more easily.

ROUNDED
Used to describe an overly full teaspoon or tablespoon measure.

SALT
A mineral that comes from both the land and the sea. Salt highlights the flavor of most ingredients, keeping foods from tasting bland.

SET ASIDE
To put food off to one side while you do something else.

SET/UNTIL SET
When a dough cooks or cools, becoming firm.

SHORTENING
A kind of solid cooking fat made from vegetable oil and used in baking.

SIFT
To pass a dry ingredient such as flour or confectioners' sugar through a sieve or sifter, to make it finer. This allows it to blend evenly with other ingredients or to be made smooth enough to decorate the surface of a cookie or brownie.

SOFTEN
To let an ingredient such as butter sit at room temperature until soft enough to spread.

SPRINKLE
To scatter one or more ingredients over a surface.

STIR
To move a utensil such as a spoon, fork, or whisk continually through ingredients, usually in a circular pattern.

SUGAR
Cooks use many different types of sugar to sweeten dishes. **Granulated sugar** is the familiar white kind, which comes in small granules that pour easily. **Brown sugar** is a kind of granulated sugar that gets its rich flavor and brown color from the addition of molasses. It is available in light and dark varieties; the dark has a stronger flavor. Because it is stickier and clumpier, brown sugar should be firmly packed down in the cup for accurate measuring. **Confectioners' sugar** is white sugar that has been ground to a fine powder and mixed with a little cornstarch to prevent clumping. It is used to make icing and for decorating desserts.

THICKEN
To add a dry ingredient such as confectioners' sugar to a mixture such as icing to make it thicker.

THIN
To add a liquid ingredient such as cream or milk to a mixture such as icing to make it more liquid.

TRIM
To cut away scraps of dough from cutout cookies, or to make dough even in shape and size.

VANILLA EXTRACT
A flavoring made from vanilla beans. Vanilla beans are the long, skinny dried seedpods of a type of orchid.

WORK SURFACE
A flat space where you can roll out dough and cut out cookies.

ZEST
The brightly colored outer layer of the peel of a citrus fruit. It is grated to add flavor to cookies and other recipes.

Index

ACKNOWLEDGMENTS

The author, Susan Manlin Katzman, would like to gratefully thank: Betty Steffen Lasky for her
invaluable help and generous contribution to this book; Hilary Skirboll for joyfully testing recipes;
and Matthew, Charlie, and Maggie for tasting cookies and inspiring sweet thoughts.

Weldon Owen would like to thank Desne Border, Ken DellaPenta, and Barbara Elliot at St. Hilary's
Parish School (Tiburon, California) for their valuable assistance in producing this book.

Special thanks to our fabulous kid models: Lee Cerre, Elizabeth Davey, Michael Dewey, Leslie Evatz, Charles Henry,
Christina Owens, Piper Patane, Terra Plumley, Billy Smith, Katie Sugarman, and Edmond Wu.

Kitchen Math

dash = 2 or 3 drops

pinch = amount you can pick up
between your thumb and forefinger

3 teaspoons = 1 tablespoon

4 tablespoons = $\frac{1}{4}$ cup

5 tablespoons + 1 teaspoon = $\frac{1}{3}$ cup

1 cup = 8 fluid ounces

2 cups = 1 pint

2 pints = 1 quart

4 quarts = 1 gallon

4 ounces = $\frac{1}{4}$ pound

8 ounces = $\frac{1}{2}$ pound

12 ounces = $\frac{3}{4}$ pound

16 ounces = 1 pound